QUICK SOLUTIONS FOR

GREAT TYPE COMBINATIONS

CAROL BUCHANAN

NORTH
LIGHT
BOOKS

CINCINNATI, OHIO

QUICK SOLUTIONS FOR

GREAT TYPE
COMBINATIONS

NORTH
LIGHT
BOOKS

CINCINNATI, OHIO

About the Author

Carol Buchanan has her own graphic design firm in Charlotte, North Carolina, specializing in publication design. She served as Art Director at F&W Publications, Inc. in Cincinnati, Ohio, for fourteen years. At F&W, she managed the in-house art department, and was responsible for book, magazine and promotion design.

Other fine Writer's Digest Books are available from your local bookstore or direct from the publisher.

98   97   96   5   4   3

Library of Congress Cataloging-in-Publication Data

Buchanan, Carol A.
    Quick solutions for great type combinations / by Carol A. Buchanan.
        p.   cm.
    Includes index.
    ISBN 0-89134-518-3
    1. Type and type-founding. 2. Printing, Practical—Layout.
I. Title.
Z250.B889 1993   93-30756
686.2'24—dc20   CIP

Edited by Mary Cropper
Designed by Clare Finney

Dedication

In memory of Mark Jacober

Acknowledgments

My thanks to Mary Cropper for her vision and support through the whole project. Also, thanks to the many talented designers willing to share their work. And finally, to the creative artists at F&W Publications whose work has been a source of inspiration.

Table of Contents

Chapter Six: Special Applications

Type considerations. Combinations for industrial and retail catalogs, menus, calendar/announcements and charts/graphs. Samples of actual printed pieces.

Chapter Seven: Using Display Type

Considerations for display type. Script, geometric, woodtype, stencil style, and digital-primitive display faces are featured. Examples of newsletters, ads, letterheads and a brochure. Samples of actual printed pieces.

Chapter Eight: Beyond the Rules

Examples of actual printed samples that show how designers are pushing the type to the limits and using type to communicate visually or emotionally........129

esign

&

ABCDEFG

TYP

12345

M

Introduction

If you're reading this book because you aren't satisfied with your ability to design with type, you are part of a very large and distinguished group. Even top designers continue to develop their talents, and have pieces with which they are not pleased. A very good designer once told me that he welcomed the opportunity to redesign a publication that he had designed several years earlier because "it...um...hadn't aged well."

This book cannot and should not be the last word on how to combine type to get a piece that's not only attractive but that's suitable for your client. It does, however, illustrate a number of combinations that do both with detailed specifications for each piece. A brief description of the client, what look was created, and the role the type plays in creating that look puts the piece into context. You may not always agree with my interpretation of a face's mood or of the look of the finished piece. Type design is a very personal thing, and what looks "friendly" to one person may look "cool" to another. The point here is to consider the effects you think you can achieve by combining typefaces.

Combinations

It's not necessary to use more than one face for a project. But when the information should or could be digested in stages, it often helps the reader to have the copy organized by a change in weight or face. A headline has very little time to attract the reader, so a large or otherwise prominent treatment of heads is logical. Subheads and captions also play a key role in attracting readers. Typically, a bold sans serif will be used for heads and subheads, a roman face for the body type, and the bold italic weight of the roman body for captions.

Since the difference between two serifs or two sans serifs of the same weight is pretty subtle, this combination usually isn't successful at organizing the copy. Even when the designer varies the weight, a type combination of all serifs or all sans serifs is difficult to bring off. (And some faces just don't look good together—Syntax with Gill Sans or Goudy with Garamond, for example.) The exception is when heads or subheads are set in a distinctive serif or sans serif display face. A cleaner, less stylized serif or sans serif that is reminiscent of the display face can be used successfully.

Trends

Great designers either appear oblivious to trends or anticipate them brilliantly. Breakthroughs that set trends are rare. Good type design can make use of fashionable typefaces and styling, but is faithful to the mission of the publication. Bad design loses sight of the mission while copying current type fashion.

Some typefaces weather well. Others suffer from overuse or misuse and fall out of favor with designers quickly. For the sample pieces created as illustrations of type combinations in this book I limited myself to about twelve typefaces plus some condensed versions, so you won't have to buy a whole type library to benefit from the ideas in this book. In choosing those core faces, I avoided those I feared wouldn't "...um...age well," and kept the list to those generally acknowledged to be classics.

Q
TUVWXYZ
123456
design
m7

About Type

Whether you sought a career designing with type, stumbled into it, or had it thrust upon you, you should realize that every day you get an education in its use from a variety of sources. Study all the printed pieces you see, and determine what makes them successful, then try to apply what you've learned to your own work.

Most of us move through design styles just as fine artists move through stylistic periods. There is some pattern to our type solutions. This is a natural evolution and reflects our personal growth. The best way to achieve that growth is to experiment, learning by trial and error not only what faces look good together, but which suit the client's needs. You will at times, however, be asked to follow a corporate style manual. Companies that build an identity with a strong corporate look will ask designers to work within previously established guidelines. But usually there's room within the guidelines for a fresh design that will be in keeping with the corporate identity.

Computers are great tools for working out an idea, but they have created some unrealistic expectations. Because they enable us to produce something typeset as quickly as it can be typewritten, schedules are compressed because there is no back and forth with the type house. It sounds simple, but you need to give yourself time to do a good type design and a good typesetting job. When you become a typesetter before you've designed the piece, you'll be frustrated with the outcome most of the time. Explore several combinations of typefaces before settling on the one you'll use. And then get the type to look right on the page.

In this chapter, we'll take a quick look at the sixteen typefaces that were used to create the examples for this book. They are Times, Palatino, Bodoni, Optima, Century, Garamond, Goudy, New Baskerville, Helvetica, Helvetica Condensed, Helvetica Compressed, Helvetica Extra Compressed, Sabon, Syntax, Futura and Futura Condensed. Futura Black, which is a stencil-style display face, is used occasionally, and several display faces are used in the chapter on display type. We'll also examine some of the factors that affect your choice of type and the various looks you can create with type.

ABCDEFGHIJKLMNOPQRSTUVWXYZ
abcdefghijklmnopqrstuvwxyz1234567890

A standard for newspapers, Times is very functional and a most economical serif for copyfitting. Because of its long association with journalism, Times is a good face to use when presenting factual material or if the copy should inspire confidence in the reader.

ABCDEFGHIJKLMNOPQRSTUVWXYZ
abcdefghijklmnopqrstuvwxyz1234567890

Palatino is more upright and less delicate than Goudy. A pretty face, it has a calligraphic quality that makes any copy look attractive. The italic (not shown here) is especially graceful and elegant. Palatino is useful when a design calls for an upscale or glamorous look.

ABCDEFGHIJKLMNOPQRSTUVWXYZ
abcdefghijklmnopqrstuvwxyz1234567890

With its thicks and thins, Bodoni is perfect for use as a headline type, but needs careful kerning. Whether condensed, expanded, all caps, or caps and lowercase, Bodoni communicates sophistication. It is not as legible for large bodies of text as less dramatic serifs .

ABCDEFGHIJKLMNOPQRSTUVWXYZ
abcdefghijklmnopqrstuvwxyz1234567890

Optima is best described as a "serifless" rather than a sans serif face. It mixes well with virtually any face, and it adds a sparkling, fresh quality to a piece. Because it is very legible, it can be used for long blocks of text if given ample white space.

ABCDEFGHIJKLMNOPQRSTUVWXYZ
abcdefghijklmnopqrstuvwxyz1234567890

A large, friendly, very legible face, Century is a good choice for small text. It reminds readers of schoolbooks, so it works when the audience is young children or parents. It also works where a large amount of information needs to be presented in a straightforward manner.

ABCDEFGHIJKLMNOPQRSTUVWXYZ
abcdefghijklmnopqrstuvwxyz1234567890

Elegant, graceful Garamond has distinctive curved serifs and old style numerals. It's an economical face—more condensed than Century or Bodoni—but still quite legible. Garamond can create a classic, timeless look or a very sophisticated one.

ABCDEFGHIJKLMNOPQRSTUVWXYZ
abcdefghijklmnopqrstuvwxyz1234567890

With more decorative flair than Garamond, Goudy is a good choice for a traditional client. This face lends itself to being set in small caps and generously tracked, which makes it a very effective display face, as well as a text face. Goudy is a light design, so it doesn't reverse as well as others.

ABCDEFGHIJKLMNOPQRSTUVWXYZ
abcdefghijklmnopqrstuvwxyz1234567890

A perfect choice for lengthy text, New Baskerville has a traditional, bookish quality. It is not boring, however, but a lively face that is a pleasure to read. It has a great distinction and delicacy that gives it presence on the page; the very attractive italic (not shown here) has warmth and charm.

ABCDEFGHIJKLMNOPQRSTUVWXYZ
abcdefghijklmnopqrstuvwxyz1234567890

A very legible sans serif, Helvetica works for a modern or contemporary project and has many useful weights. Its universal character makes it easy to use in a wide variety of applications. In the bold and black weights (not shown here) it makes headlines dynamic and forceful.

ABCDEFGHIJKLMNOPQRSTUVWXYZ
abcdefghijklmnopqrstuvwxyz1234567890

Helvetica remains very legible even when condensed, and the condensed version is available in many weights. This makes it a good choice for long captions set on a narrow measure and other situations in which space may be at a premium. In the bold and black weights especially (not shown here) it stands out clearly on the page; this makes it a good choice for long subheads in narrow columns or for calling out small bits of information.

ABCDEFGHIJKLMNOPQRSTUVWXYZ
abcdefghijklmnopqrstuvwxyz1234567890

Helvetica Compressed is an even more condensed version of Helvetica. The letterforms have been greatly condensed, which makes the internal spaces much smaller and the type much darker. Use this carefully, or you may emphasize an element with the type color when you don't mean to. This face will benefit from generous leading and loose tracking.

ABCDEFGHIJKLMNOPQRSTUVWXYZ
abcdefghijklmnopqrstuvwxyz1234567890

Helvetica Extra Compressed is more condensed than Helvetica Compressed. It is still legible, but it does get tiring to read and should be avoided for long blocks of copy. It is, however, quite useful for fairly long captions. You will need to set the tracking loosely for readabililty.

ABCDEFGHIJKLMNOPQRSTUVWXYZ
abcdefghijklmnopqrstuvwxyz1234567890

A good text face, Sabon is less economical than New Baskerville. In all caps, it is classic, and less common than Garamond. This face has attractive, very calligraphic letterforms that lend interest to any page. The italic (not shown here) has quirky, charming letterforms but is quite legible.

ABCDEFGHIJKLMNOPQRSTUVWXYZ
abcdefghijklmnopqrstuvwxyz1234567890

Syntax has a casual, chiseled quality perfect where a casual sans serif is needed. It has more movement and spontaneity than most other sans serifs due to the calligraphic quality of its letterforms. It can be used for text as well as display purposes, but it does need ample white space for legibility.

ABCDEFGHIJKLMNOPQRSTUVWXYZ
abcdefghijklmnopqrstuvwxyz1234567890

A delicate, round, sans serif, Futura can be classic or contemporary. Futura has a wide range of weights that are very useful. All of the weights have excellent round proportions.

ABCDEFGHIJKLMNOPQRSTUVWXYZ
abcdefghijklmnopqrstuvwxyz1234567890

A must for ad work, Futura Extra Bold has a lot of weight and impact for headlines and subheads. It also works well for very graphic initial caps. The condensed version shown here is exceptionally legible and useful in applications where space is at a premium, such as ads.

Type Tips

The type combinations in this book are not the only solutions for the projects, but offer a method of arriving at appropriate combinations. When you approach a type design, look at the whole project, including format, audience and message, instead of trying to find a serif and a sans serif that "go together." Certain "givens" will set clear parameters for both format and type decisions.

The format of a piece is determined by where it will be seen and how it will be used. Letterhead must fit into a standard-size envelope, and brochures generally need to fit into a file drawer. How much copy must be fit into the piece and how the audience will read it also affects type choice, as does the age and interest level of potential readers. The message and the mood that reinforce that message are another major consideration since these greatly affect the look of a piece.

The average reader may not be able to differentiate between two serifs or recognize the names of the fonts, but will be affected by the mood they convey. The choice of the body and headline type make the clearest mood statement. The accent face, usually a sans serif, makes its statement with placement, weight and style. Do you want to give the consumer what he expects? For purposes of this book, I'm assuming the answer is, generally, "Yes." The ad design appropriate for a rock radio station or pet store will not enhance the reputation of a hospital or law firm. Once you have determined the look you need, you're ready to start designing. Here are a few guidelines for creating several typical looks for clients.

Conservative, Traditional. A conservative approach calls for all things in moderation, including size, leading (not too generous, not too tight), kerning and tracking (ditto), horizontal scale, column measure and weight. Some serif fonts, Goudy for instance, are naturals for a conservative mood, but all work when styled conservatively. The accent face should not be an extreme weight, a bold rather than a black. Assuming a normal two- or three-column measure, Helvetica, Futura or Optima in their regular or bold weights add variety to a mainly serif approach without making too much of a graphic statement.

Trendy, Graphic. The graphic approach to typography is defined by the interplay between black and white. Bauer Bodoni is a natural for trendy, graphic body copy. It's not the most legible body face, but the thicks and thins in its letters keep the black and white play going. Generously leading a black or extra black sans serif doesn't enhance legibility, but it does make a bold graphic pattern and provide relief from a gray page of text. You may use a condensed sans serif, even an extra compressed. Generously tracked letters, especially an extra bold geometric font like Futura Extra Bold set in caps, also create a patchwork of black and white. There is lots of variety in weights, ultra thins and extra bolds.

Romantic, Nostalgic. This typographic treatment is similar to that for a traditional look. The romantic message is reinforced with the use of italics or a script display face. A serif with flourish, like Palatino, is a natural for body copy. (Palatino also has a lovely, scriptlike italic.) For a more nostalgic look, a face with an old-fashioned character, such as Goudy, helps set an appropriate mood. The accent face should be light and airy, perhaps Futura, generously leaded or kerned, or Optima, which is softer and less geometric than the other sans serifs.

Naive, Playful. Size plays an important part in a naive or playful type design. Century used at a slightly larger size as body type reminds the reader of school books. In general, an upper- and lowercase setting of an open face with a large x-height has a direct, childlike quality. Syntax has more flair than Helvetica for an accent type, but both work well for the playful layout. Lean toward display type that is simple, fun and geometric (like Baby Teeth or Stencil).

High Tech, Futuristic. A condensed sans serif is a possibility for body copy. Keep the layout clean. Instead of changing emphasis with size and weight, vary only the weight. Use a condensed, generously leaded serif like Garamond or Sabon in a narrow measure for variety. Place short copy blocks in white space or reverse them out of black to simulate a star or planet in open space.

Natural, Homespun. The primary font should be a serif like Goudy or Garamond, set in uppercase and lowercase or set in small caps for headlines. Garamond, slightly condensed and tightly tracked, is a good choice for a headline. The accent face should be used sparingly. Syntax Ultra Black has a chiseled quality. Try leading and tracking the accent face generously to simulate park signage chiseled in wood.

Glossary

Baseline. The invisible guideline upon which the characters of a typeset line, except the descenders, appear to sit.

Body. The main copy or the text of a printed piece.

Callout. This term is used instead of pull quote by many designers. See *pull quote*.

Caps. Usually written with a small *c*. Type that is set in all uppercase or capital letters.

Caption. The copy that accompanies and explains a visual.

Color. The lightness or darkness of an area of type.

Compressed. A typeface with characters designed to be narrower than the condensed version of that type family. See also *condensed*.

Condensed. A typeface with characters designed to be narrower than the width of the characters of the regular weight in that type family.

Dingbat. An ornamental symbol used for emphasis or decoration. The set of Zapf Dingbats is available on many computers and printers; special sets of other typographic ornaments can also be purchased.

Display Type. Type set larger than the copy, generally eighteen points or larger, that is intended to catch a reader's attention.

Expanded. A typeface with characters that are designed to be wider than the regular weight of that type family.

Folio. A page number.

Font. A single weight and design of a given typeface, including caps and lowercase letters, numerals, fractions (if available), accented characters and punctuation. See also *typeface*.

Header. Copy that appears at the top (or head) of each page.

Headline. Most important level of information; intended to summarize copy and attract attention. Set in display type. (See *display type*.)

Horizontal Scaling. Manually altering the width of the characters in a typeface to make them set wider or narrower; usually expressed as a percentage.

Initial Cap. Enlarged letter at the beginning of a block of copy or line of display type.

Italic. Type in which the letters are slanted to the right; generally drawn to suggest handwriting. Although any type slanted to the right is often called italic, type that slants to the right but retains the characteristics of the regular style is technically termed

"oblique," and you may need to order a font using that term.

Kerning. Adjusting the spacing between individual pairs of letters.

Lead-in. Setting the first words of a paragraph in italic, boldface or all caps for emphasis or organization.

Leading. The distance from the baseline of one line of type to the line above it.

Letterform. The shape of the letter, the unique characteristics of its strokes.

Masthead. The title of a newsletter, also called a nameplate, banner or logo.

Measure. The length of a line of type.

Old Style Numerals. Numerals that have ascenders and descenders. The numeral *1* is often written as *I* instead of the arabic numeral.

Pull Quote. Also called a *callout*. A statement or quotation excerpted from an article that is set in display or with some other decorative type treatment to attract attention.

Reverse(d) Type. White or light-colored letters set on a dark background.

Small Caps. Uppercase letters that are about 60 percent of the full cap height used in place of lowercase letters for effect.

Subhead. Secondary level of heading, usually located between the headline and the copy or between sections of the copy.

Tagline. Descriptive copy set with a logotype.

Tracking. Adjusting the spacing between all characters evenly. Page layout programs express this differently. The samples in this book were created with QuarkXPress, which allows you to add or subtract units of space in fairly small increments. This figure has been written as "tracking: +1" or "tracking -12".

Typeface. A named type design, such as Goudy, Garamond or Optima.

Type Family. Complete set of styles and weights for a single typeface.

Type Style. The variations of a typeface. Italic and outline versions are type styles; different weights, such as bold, are often considered styles or styling.

Violator. A short block of text set apart for emphasis, often at an angle or "stamped" into body copy.

X-Height. The height of lowercase letters, excluding the ascenders and descenders.

design &

ABCDE

TY

M

1234

Newsletters

Many designers get their first opportunity to do corporate work with a newsletter project, but it isn't always an easy job. The budgets are usually tight, and design considerations take a back seat to the piece's function as a communication tool. The amount of copy fluctuates from issue to issue and often comes in late. The editor of the typical newsletter is either an overworked personnel coordinator or an administrator with little editorial experience who must squeeze writing a newsletter into an already full day.

The content and length of the article depends on the type of newsletter. A small company's employee newsletter relies on employee submissions, which are usually short and include choppy lists of elements such as birth announcements and bowling scores. The challenge here isn't to make it lively, but to clean up and organize the disparate elements.

A larger company or institution with a communications department may use its house organ to disseminate long, dry, informational articles to employees, stockholders, alumni, etc. Here, the challenge is to make the information visually interesting without a budget for quality photography or illustration.

Type Considerations

Legibility is an important consideration. What is the age and education level of the audience? For example, older individuals may have physical difficulty reading, so you'll need to choose a very legible face and set it fairly large. A serif type with a large x-height is a good choice for the body type. If there are long, chatty captions with photographs, and you know these captions have a high level of readership, make the captions prominent and legible. Where you must run long, dry material, use pull quotes to pique curiosity.

Remember that, unlike with an ad or billboard, your audience will be spending time with this material, and is probably predisposed to read it. So you won't need blaring headlines. The exception is the newsletter that will be displayed in common areas more like a poster, or where the editorial thrust is to ape tabloids or present "hot flash" bulletins. Usually the latter occurs when the newsletter is actually a promotion piece.

Since your audience is small and perceives the newsletter as having some value, encourage loyalty by having a consistent typographic look. Display elements like new visuals, the table of contents, and a change of the second color to alert the reader that this is a new issue.

Copy Heavy & Attractive

This client wanted an attractive newsletter packed with information. The amount of copy planned for each issue dictated either a three- or four-column format. The four-column format was chosen because it gives greater flexibility in photo sizing. Newsletters often have poor quality photos because they rely on amateur photographers, so some photos may have to be run very small to hide their defects—an easier task with a four-column grid.

This classic magazine look will help meet the goal of making this copy-heavy newsletter attractive. The information is not short and choppy; it may run throughout several columns. Times Roman is a classic serif font with a low x-height that works well for the body copy in this narrow column format. Large initial caps set in Times will give the newsletter a magazine feel and open up the long blocks of copy a little. Pull quotes, which are also set in Times, provide visual variety within the editorial look.

Masthead: Times Roman 96/19, horizontal scaling: 85%, and Futura Extra Bold 12/19, tracking: +18
Heads: Times Roman 48 pt.
Subheads: Futura Extra Bold 11/13
Initial Caps and Callouts: Times Roman 18/24
Body: Times Roman 11/13
Captions: Times Roman Bold Italic 11/13

Slick, Corporate

For this client, a provider of health care services to large corporations, the newsletter needs a slick, corporate look. Using the extra bold weight of Futura has been a popular approach to corporate design, because you can emphasize with weight only, not size. The headline is only 18-point type, but the extra bold weight prevents it from getting lost on the page. Garamond body, with its large x-height type, is very legible, and makes the publication more inviting than a sans serif body type would. Its graceful appearance makes it an interesting contrast to solidly assertive Futura.

This unusual headline treatment works here because there's only one headlined article on the page, and the combination of the Futura Extra Bold type and the visual give the headline enough punch to stand out. This treatment is most effective when you have a well-organized page with only one or two articles. If there are several short articles on a page, an asymmetrical approach like this can backfire and leave readers guessing what headline goes with which article.

Masthead: Futura Extra Bold and Futura, both 40 pt.
Heads: Futura Extra Bold 18 pt.
Subheads: Futura Extra Bold 11/14
Initial Caps: Futura Extra Bold 24 pt.
Body: Garamond 11/14
Captions: Futura 9/14

HealthCareNews

Hypnosis On Trial

Extensive clinical trials to test use of hypnosis for pain relief to begin soon

Lorem ipsum dolor sit amet, al consectetuer adipiscing elit, sed diam nonummy nibh euismod ut tincidunt ut laoreet dolore sed magna aliquam erat volutpat. Ut wisi enim ad minim veniam, quis nostrud exerci tation ullam nec corper suscipit lobortis nisl ut aliquip ex ea commodo corpo et consequat.

Duis autem vel eum iriure dolor in hendrerit in vulputate velit esse molestie consequat, vel illum dolore eu feugiat nulla facilisis at vero eros et atque est numquam accumsan et iusto al odio dignissim qui blandit benin praesent luptatum zzril delenit augue duis dolore te feugait num nulla facilisi.

Lorem ipsum dolor sit amet, consectetuer adipiscing elit, sed diam nonummy nibh euismod tincidunt ut laoreet dolore quod magna aliquam erat volutpat. et Lorem ipsum dolor sit amet, sed consectetuer adipiscing elit, sed diam nonummy nibh euismod tincidunt ut laoreet dolore nunc tamquam valore erat volutpat.

This laboratory will be the setting for the clinical trials of the new hypnosis therapy. Those who are undergoing therapy can also enjoy the benfits of the lovely gardens at the institute. It should be a pleasant experience.

Rising Costs Studied

Panel to review procedures and make extensive recommendations

Lorem ipsum dolor sit amet, et consectetuer adipiscing elit, sed diam nonummy nibh euismod tincidunt ut laoreet dolore est magna aliquam erat volutpat. Ut wisi enim ad minim veniam, quis nostrud exerci tation corper erat

Risl ut aliquip ex ea nihil est commodo consequat. Duis aus autem vel eum iriure dolor in hendrerit in vulputate velit esse molestie consequat, vel illum et dolore eu feugiat nulla facilisis at vero eros et accumsan et.

Iusto odio dignissim qui et blandit praesent luptatum zzril delenit augue duis dolore te alia feugait nulla facilisi. Lorem ipso ipsum dolor sit amet, consect etuer adipiscing elit, sed diam nonumny nibh euismod quod tincidunt ut laoreet dolore est.

HealthCare *Communique*

 D uis autem atque vellum eum est iriure dolores in hendressrit inqui vulputate velit esse eius molestie consequat, vel os illum dolore eu fugitatum feugiat nullam facilisis at vero eros et accumsan et iusto odio dignissim qui blandit praesent

luptatum zzril delenit augue duis dolore te aus feugait nulla tumm quam facilisi. Lorem ipsum et dolor sit amet, consect et etuer adipiscing elit, sed diam nonummy nibh sed euismod tincidunt utque laoreet dolore magnam et aliquam erat volutpat. est tam Lorem ipsum dolore sit amet, consectetuer et ipso adipis kcing elit, sed diam nonummy nibh.

euismod tincidunt ut laoreet dolore magnam et aliquam erat volutpat. Ut wisi enim ad minim tum veniam, quis nostrud sed num exerci tation benigne ullamcorper suscipit est lobortis nisl ut aliquip ex ea commodo consequat. Duis autem vel leussm ex iriure dolore in hendrerit in vulputate velit esse oar molestie consequat, velo

Hypnosis On Trial

illum dolores eius feugiat nulla facilisis at vero eros et accumsan et iusto odio dignissim qui blandit praesent luptatum zzril delenit augue duis dolore te feugait nulla facilisi.

New Anaesthetic
Lorem ipsum dolor sit

amet, consectetuer adipo iscing elit, sed et diaming nonummy nibh euismod extincidunt ut laoreet qui dolore magna aliquam et erat volutpat. Lorem ipis ipsum dolores sit ammet, consectetuer adipiscing elit, sed diam nonummy nibh euismod extincidunt

ut laoreet dolore magnam aliquam erat volutpat. Ut wisi enim ad minim aliqu veniam, quis nossstrud al exerci tation ullamcorper suscipit lobrrortis nisl ut aliquip ex ea commmodo consequat. Duis autem et vel eum iriure dolores in hendrerit in vulputate ex

Lorem ipsum dolore sit amet, consectetuer et ipso adipis kcing elit, sed diam nonummy nibh. ipsum dolore sit amet, consectetuer et ipso adipis kcing elit, sed diam nonummy ni. ipsum dolore sit amet, consectetuer et ipso adipis kcing elit, sed diam nonummy ni.

Basic, Friendly

Century and Helvetica are used here for a very basic, legible newsletter. This look would be right for a newsletter with basic childcare information, or one for a primary audience of older adults. Because both Century and Helvetica have an open, schoolbook primer quality, they fit comfortably together here. The three-column format has a longer line length for legibility than a four-column format would. This is important since neither Century nor Helvetica is economical.

The larger Helvetica subheads pull the reader into the article. The type follows a clear hierarchy: The heads have the most emphasis—they're set in a heavy weight of a contrasting typeface and are almost twice as large as the subheads. The subheads get most of their emphasis from the extra leading. They fall squarely between the weight of the head and the body copy, creating a clear visual sense of what readers should read first, second and third.

Masthead: Century 96 pt.
Heads: Helvetica Extra Bold 30/34
Subheads: Helvetica 18/30
Body: Century 11/15
Captions: Helvetica 11/15

Soft-Sell, Editorial

Optima and Palatino have a softer effect that's right for a newsletter dealing primarily with women's health care issues. You don't have to hit anyone over the head with the headlines because the benefit in reading this helpful information is obvious. The headline is subtly emphasized by a change of typeface and the large amount of white space setting it off from other elements on the page.

Health care organizations' newsletters usually have longer editorial and a few human interest photos. Italic captions and soft shadow boxes behind the initial caps work well with this soft-sell, editorial approach. In addition to their purely decorative function, initial caps guide the reader. They should not be too distracting in a low-key layout, but their effect can be softened with the use of screens or color. They establish a starting point and break up unrelated blocks of copy. As a general rule try to allow as much space to the right of the cap as you leave below it.

Masthead: Optima 72 pt. and Palatino Italic 60 pt.
Heads: Optima 30/34
Subheads: Optima 11/15
Captions: Palatino Italic 9/15
Body: Palatino 11/15
Initial Caps: Palatino 36 pt.

No-Nonsense

This no-nonsense newsletter is aimed at investors as well as employees, with a factual account of the company's and the industry's news. A column of justified type looks more serious than one set rag right, and in this three-column format the Futura doesn't break badly.

Body copy is usually set in a serif with a sans serif for visual variety. Here the serif, Sabon, in an italic breaks up the sans serif Futura body copy. Futura is a strong, legible typeface and when set with open leading as done here is quite readable. It also looks no-nonsense and restrained. The slightly quirky Sabon italic adds a lively accent without disturbing the overall look of the piece.

The left column is used for the masthead and a table of contents. This airy approach provides relief from a gray page with no illustrations and lends emphasis to the delicate masthead.

Masthead: Sabon 38/58, tracking: -5
Heads: Sabon Italic 18/24
Body: Futura 12/15, justified
Table of Contents: Futura 18/24

Graphic, Corporate

A five-column grid with at least one open column in which only captions and graphics will appear adds interest to this corporate newsletter. In addition to visual interest, the narrower column format also solves the problem of coping with head shots. Remember, headshots shouldn't be too large.

Syntax Ultra Black has a little more flair than Helvetica for the masthead, but a condensed Helvetica is needed for bold heads that won't break badly in this narrow format. The Garamond Italic contrasts with the Syntax and adds a warm, conversational quality to captions that have high readership.

Masthead: Syntax and Syntax Ultra Black, both 54 pt.
Heads: Helvetica Black Condensed 18/24
Subheads: Helvetica Condensed 10/15
Captions: Garamond Italic 10/15
Body: Syntax 10/15

Informal, Friendly

This is a homier approach to a corporate newsletter. The Sabon Bold Italic body type set flush left suggests a handwritten letter. Although the rule says that you can't set whole pages in italic, here it looks casual and friendly—and is comfortable to read. The loose leading gives it breathing room and all the articles are short, so readers won't tire before they reach the end of one. The letter from the editor in the upper left-hand corner is an important part of the personal letter feeling the client wants to project. It is given emphasis with the large drop cap.

Because the body is run in a bold italic, this copy would still be very legible in a color other than black. For a traditional look on a gritty, recycled sheet, the type could run in two dark, earth colors. The narrow column of text, which is set caption-like at the top of the page, could be volume number and dateline information, company slogan, or brief introductory copy.

Futura Bold captions draw the reader's attention, and with their added weight will be legible in a second color.

Masthead: Sabon Italic, "The" 42 pt., "Old Saw" 96 pt.
Publication Information: Sabon Italic 14/24
Heads: Sabon Italic 18/24
Initial Caps: Sabon Italic 48 pt.
Captions: Futura Bold 9/16
Body: Sabon Bold Italic 11/16

Factual, Journalistic

This newsletter is devoted to informing the company's stockholders and other investors about industry trends and company business developments. The no-nonsense design enhances the credibility of the information. Although this newsletter is sent outside the company, the word *News*, rather than the company name, is typographically emphasized in the masthead. Also note the contrast between the old-fashioned, dignified quality of the Bauer Bodoni, which suggests the character of the company, and the hard-edged, modern look of the Futura, which is used to suggest urgency and immediacy. This reinforces the idea that readers are getting news and not just public relations fluff. This approach works because the primary audience is investors who know what Steel Tek is.

The design borrows from newspapers the bold reversed mast and heavy sans serif heads. A column of Bodoni, one of the classic newspaper faces, reinforces the newspaper feel.

Masthead: Bauer Bodoni and Futura Extra Bold 82 pt.
Heads: Futura Extra Bold 24/26, tracking: -5
Captions: Futura Bold 9/15
Body: Bauer Bodoni 11/15
Subheads: Futura Bold 12/15, tracking: -2

Fresh, Magazine-like

While pretty straightforward, this newsletter takes some features from contemporary magazine design to give it a fresh look. The light and heavy weights of Futura are heavily leaded and set on a shorter measure for heads and subheads to leave some white space for a more graphic look. (Also note that the change from head to subhead is handled by changing only the weight of the typeface, but that's enough.) The Palatino body copy is also generously leaded and run flush left, rag right.

The *BA&A* in the masthead reflects the design of the company's logo. Its chunkiness is balanced by the large, flowing letterforms of *Report*. Because the publication information needs to be kept small so as not to detract from the masthead's overall design, it too has been set in Futura, which reverses out well in small sizes.

Masthead: Palatino Italic 96 pt., and Futura and Futura Extra Bold 48 pt.
Publication Information: Futura 10/12
Heads: Futura Extra Bold 16/25
Table of Contents: Futura and Futura Extra Bold, both 16/25
Subheads: Futura 16/25
Body: Palatino 11/17

Lighthearted

This accountant's newsletter takes a lighthearted approach to communicating tax and other information. The reversed pull quotes and heavy use of rules (between columns and as a border) have a seed package effect that suits the newsletter's name and image well. Goudy has an old-fashioned, chiseled look that keeps the newsletter from being too cute, and contrasts well with Futura Extra Bold heads set in all caps. The Futura Extra Bold offers a nice contrast to the old-fashioned text face, and saves the newsletter from being too prim and fussy.

Goudy has a small x-height, so it's condensed slightly for display heads like the masthead and pull quote. The bold italic weight holds up well when reversed; the regular italic weight would have been too hard to read. Futura, especially, has a dramatically different effect in different weights. The Goudy Bold Italic captions echo the callouts and are beefy enough to run in a second color.

Masthead: Goudy 80 pt.
Heads: Futura Extra Bold 14/25, caps
Subheads: Futura 16/25
Captions: Goudy Bold Italic 9/15
Pull Quote: Goudy Bold Italic 16/20
Body: Goudy 11/17

Official

Times Roman is a natural for a clean, news-oriented publication. Helvetica Bold subheads have less visual impact than the extra black weight of Futura Extra Bold, but the visual statement is made here by the prominent use of Times Roman.

The carefully kerned and centered Times is reminiscent of an official government document. This look conveys a feeling of urgency and importance to Bailey Arnold's clients. The official look is carried through with heavy bars over the heads, and the justified columns. When centering heads of varying lengths, a bar of the full column(s) measure helps maintain the grid. The treatment of the bars over the heads is picked up for the masthead with a twist. The company name is reversed out of the heavy bar, which gives it enough weight to have equal emphasis with the title.

Masthead: Helvetica caps 16 pt. and Times Roman 110 pt.
Heads: Times Roman 60 pt.
Subheads: Helvetica Bold 18/24, centered
Captions: Helvetica Extra Bold 9/15
Body: Times Roman 12/15

Kept for Reference

Some newsletters are intended to be saved in a binder, so the inside margin must be deep to allow for hole-punching. The resulting narrower image area makes a two-column format a good solution. The wide columns can be divided for flexibility, as shown here, for photos, captions and other visual elements.

The information being presented is not bulletin-like, but reference material. This is reinforced by modest head size and weight. The overall look is rather conservative and scholarly, reflecting the newsletter's role as an informative reference document. The readable and dignified Sabon body copy is well suited for that type of look. To keep it from looking too dry and dusty, Optima has been used in a regular and a bold weight because it's friendlier than Helvetica or Futura.

Masthead: Optima and Optima Bold 42 pt.
Heads: Optima Bold 24/25
Captions: Optima Bold and Optima, both 9/11
Body: Sabon 11/15
Byline: Optima Italic 11/15

Copy Light & Rhythmic

White space, which balances the text, and the choppy, generously leaded bold heads, subheads and captions make this newsletter fun to read. An arts organization newsletter generally has short pieces of copy about openings and other events. The Futura Extra Bold attracts the reader's eye to the headline and allows the reader to hop around and read the articles and announcements of interest. Bauer Bodoni, with its thicks and thins, sacrifices some readability but makes for a very graphic presentation. Very generous leading for display elements continues the choppy rhythm of black and white play between type and white space.

The masthead has a bouncy rhythm that balances the more delicate Bodoni with generously tracked, smaller, heavier Futura Extra Bold. Emphasis is placed on the word *Art*, something the readers relate to and support, with placement, size, and a change of face.

Masthead: Bauer Bodoni 120 pt., and Futura Extra Bold caps 14 pt., tracking: +12
Publication Information: Bauer Bodoni 24 pt.
Heads: Bauer Bodoni 24/28
Subheads: Futura Extra Bold 11/25
Captions: Futura Extra Bold 8/17
Body: Bauer Bodoni 10/15

Restrained, Bauhaus

A more rigid, but still flexible, approach is taken here. The emphasis in the masthead is achieved with tracking and weight—a clean, graphic approach. Although this is less of a fun look than many arts organizations newsletters have, it's a good, restrained, "art" look in the classic Bauhaus tradition. It would be most appropriate for a more traditional, conservative institution.

The Helvetica Black Condensed heads and captions are generously leaded for emphasis, but run in the same point size as the body. This solution to emphasizing copy is less predictable and more sophisticated than mixing sizes and weights.

Masthead: Helvetica Condensed 50 pt., tracking: +42, and Helvetica Black Condensed 50 pt.
Heads: Helvetica Black Condensed 11/25
Subheads: Helvetica Condensed 11/17
Captions: Helvetica Black Condensed 8/17
Body: Sabon 11/15

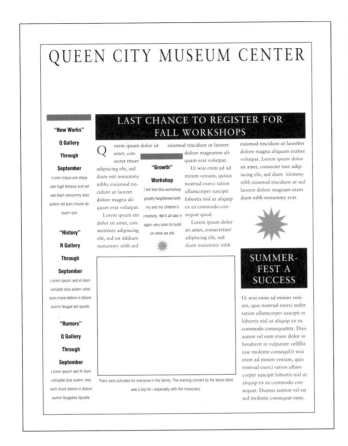

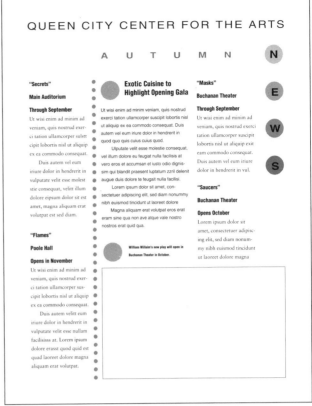

Classic & Fun

An arts organization newsletter can be classic and fun at the same time, so it can attract both conservative potential sponsors and young members with families. Sabon is condensed and generously tracked for a classic look. Sabon is a classic typeface with traditional letterforms and chiseled serifs, and the masthead has been given a traditional setting—slightly condensed and generously tracked.

The fun begins with the all cap serif heads reversed out of bars, complemented by simple graphic icons of the sun, run in a screen of black or a second color. Shorter, bulletin-like material is set centered on a narrow column (another classic typographic approach) to add a strong graphic accent from the patterns created by the lines of type and the white space. This narrow column dictates a legible condensed font, such as the Helvetica Black Condensed and Helvetica Condensed used here, for the heads and copy.

Masthead: Sabon caps 34 pt., horizontal scaling: 80%, tracking: +25
Heads: Sabon caps 18/28, tracking: +12
Subheads: Helvetica Black Condensed 11/25
Pull Quotes: Helvetica Black Condensed and Helvetica Condensed, both 8/17
Body: Sabon 10/15 and Helvetica Condensed 8/17
Initial Caps: Sabon 24 pt.
Captions: Helvetica Condensed 8/17

Modern, Urban

Although this newsletter for a performing arts center uses the same typefaces as the first one on this page, the look is completely different. Helvetica set all caps (slightly expanded, and generously tracked) provides a sophisticated, understated approach for the masthead, while Helvetica Black Condensed is a weightier solution for heads and subheads. Notice how the heads clearly dominate the generously leaded subheads, not with drastically larger proportions, but with tighter leading to enhance their weight.

The Sabon body type is made more interesting by the generous leading. A wider column accommodates the longer feature articles. For variety, this copy is set in downsized Helvetica with the same leading as the Sabon.

Masthead: Helvetica Expanded 20 pt., horizontal scaling: 120%, tracking: +22, and Helvetica Bold 20 pt., horizontal scaling: 120%, tracking: +22 (NEWS)
Issue Date: Helvetica 16 pt., manual letterspacing
Heads: Helvetica Black Condensed 14/16
Subheads: Helvetica Black Condensed 11/25
Pull Quotes: Helvetica Black Condensed 11/25
Body: Sabon 10/17 and Helvetica 9/15
Captions: Helvetica Black Condensed 7/15

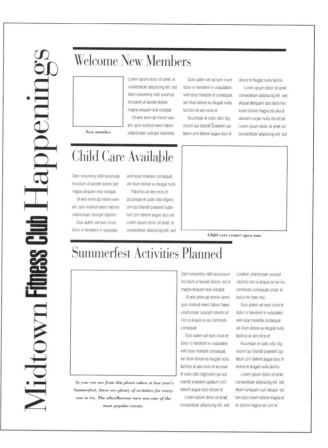

Attracting Attention

This newsletter is aimed at the club's young (roughly ages twenty-one to thirty) members, who are more likely to flip through it than to read it. It features some previously published general health and fitness information in order to flesh out an otherwise choppy calendar of events. The four-column grid allows for more use of photos.

The design borrows some attention-getting features of magazine and ad design to help pull the readers in. The treatment of the "Health Watch" article is similar to a magazine format. Ditto the bold initial cap. The condensed and tightly kerned Garamond masthead is ad-like, especially the "New" violator. The Futura Extra Bold holds up well when reversed and gives needed emphasis to the captions—skimming readers want to check out the pictures and captions first—and the motto without overpowering the primary elements of the design.

Masthead: Garamond 96 pt.
Violator: Futura Extra Bold 48 pt.
Motto: Futura Extra Bold 12/18
Department Head: Futura Extra Bold caps 11/17
Heads: Garamond 36/30 and Futura Extra Bold caps 11/17
Captions: Futura Extra Bold caps 9/17
Body: Garamond 11/17
Initial Cap: Futura Extra Bold 24 pt.

Sophisticated, Graphic

This newsletter targeted to sophisticated, urban professionals relies on club happenings and photos for its content. The layout is graphic, allowing lots of options for photo sizing. The audience for this publication is generally young, so legibility is not a primary concern. The overall look is less editorial than calendar-like. The masthead that runs down the length of the front page is borrowed from calendar layout.

The Helvetica Bold Condensed body type works here because the approach is graphic and the articles are short. Otherwise, legibility would be an issue. Bauer Bodoni is a natural for an urban, sophisticated look. The Bauer Bodoni heads are tightly kerned and condensed for emphasis, and receive further emphasis from heavy rules. The captions are emphasized by the heavy leading and the white space created by centering them under each photo.

Masthead: Bauer Bodoni and Helvetica Compressed Black, both 60 pt.
Heads: Bauer Bodoni Condensed 30 pt.
Captions: Bauer Bodoni Italic 9/15
Body: Helvetica Bold Condensed 9/15

A Retail Look

Fitness clubs compete for the same market—young adults who want to improve their appearance and meet members of the opposite sex. This means their newsletters all need to have short blocks of copy and lots of photos and could easily look like a bunch of clones. To stand out from the crowd, the overall look reflects retail merchandising; the compressed lettering and centered format are borrowed from hang tags in clothing stores.

The body copy carries out the theme. This would be tiresome to read if there were a lot of copy, but it's fine for short text blocks. Heads are in Helvetica Ultra Compressed, so they'll have a strong presence on the page but still fit the narrow columns and be legible. Ultra compressed faces are trendy and impactful, another retail fashion device. The captions are Times Italic because there will be a high level of readership for the chatty captions. Awkward spaces left by short copy are filled with tilted callouts in Helvetica Compressed.

Masthead: Helvetica Black Compressed 60 pt.
Heads: Helvetica Black Compressed 24/30
Callouts: Helvetica Black Compressed 18/24
Captions: Times Roman Italic 9/15
Body: Times Roman 11/15, centered

"Pumping Iron" Look

A traditional three-column format and beefy masthead works for a club whose membership is primarily businessmen. The "Club News" stamp plays on a connection to crate stamps and safaris—a sort of "he-man," macho look. The initial caps in Bodoni Bold carry through the crate stencil look.

Bodoni says "business" and the Syntax Ultra Black is rounder than Futura Extra Bold but just as strong. The rounder quality makes it more distinctive for the masthead and reinforces the "pumping iron" connection. Bold sans serifs like Syntax Ultra have been popularized in packaging, including vitamins and other medicines, so there's a subliminal reinforcement. The contrast in faces, tracking, and overall treatment emphasizes the benefit of joining the club while keeping the club name in front of the reader.

Masthead: Syntax Ultra Black 120 pt., and Bodoni 36 pt., tracking: +26
Heads: Syntax Ultra Black 18/27
Subheads: Syntax 11/27
Captions: Syntax 9/13
Initial Caps: Bodoni Bold 36/16
Body: Bodoni Bold 11/16
Club News Stamp: Bodoni Bold caps 24/28

The ATHENEUM Quarterly
FALL

LIBRARY CONSTRUCTION UPDATE

The new wing ipsum dolor sit amet, consectetuer adipiscing elit, sed diam nonummy nibh euismod tincidunt ut laoreet dolore magna aliquam erat volutpat.

Ut wisi enim ad minim veniam, quis nostrud exerci tation ullamcorper suscipit lobortis nisl ut aliquip ex ea commodo consequat.

Duis autem vel eum iriure dolor in hendrerit in vulputate velit esse molestie consequat, vel illum dolore eu feugait nulla facilisis at vero eros et accumsan et iusto odio dignissim qui blandit praesent luptatum zzril delenit augue duis dolore te feugait nulla facilisi.

Lorem ipsum dolor sit amet, consectetuer adipiscing elit, sed diam nonummy nibh euismod tincidunt ut laoreet dolore magna aliquam erat volutpat.

Lorem ipsum dolor sit amet, consectetuer adipiscing elit, sed diam nonummy nibh euismod tin-

cidunt ut laoreet dolore magna aliquam erat volutpat. Nihil nisi bonum quod ipso facto erat num.

Ut wisi enim ad minim veniam, quis nostrud exerci tation ullamcorper suscipit lobortis erat nisl ut aliquip ex ea commodo consequat.

Duis autem vel eum iriure dolor in hendrerit in vulputate velit esse molestie consequat, vel

illum dolore eu feugiat nulla facilisis at vero eros et accumsan et iusto odio dignissim qui blandit

praesent luptatum et delenit augue et dolore te feugait facilis volutpat fugit fugis est.

The new wing will provide stack space for 30,000 books and fifty more carrels.

ALUMNI NEWS

A member of the class ipsum dolor sit amet, consectetuer adipiscing elit, sed diam nonummy nibh euismod tincidunt ut laoreet dolore magna aliquam erat volutpat.

Ut wisi enim ad minim veniam, quis nostrud exerci tation

ullamcorper suscipit lobortis nisl ut aliquip ex ea commodo consequat ullamcorper.

Duis autem vel eum iriure dolor in hendrerit in vulputate velit nulla facilisis at vero eros et accumsan euismod tincidunt ut laoreeterat volutpat.

Atheneum*News*

LIBRARY CONSTRUCTION UPDATE

Lorem ipsum dolor sit amet, consectetuer adipiscing elit, sed diam nonummy nibh euismod est tincidunt ut laoreet dolore magna aliquam erat volutpat. Ut wisi et enim ad minim veniam, quis nostrud exerci tation ullamcorperum suscipit lobortis nisl ut aliquip ex ea commodo consequat.

Duis autem vel eum iriure nis dolor in hendrerit in vulputatetal velit esse molestie consequat, vel illum dolore eu feugiat nulla num facilisis at vero eros et accumsan et iusto odio dignissim qui bland-it praesent luptatum zzril delenit augue duis dolore te feugait nulla facilisi. Lorem ipsum dolor sit et amet, consectetuer adipiscingtam elit, sed diam nonummy nibh nil euismod tincidunt ut laoreet quo dolore magna aliquam erat volut-pat.

Lorem ipsum dolor sit amet, consectetuer adipiscing elit, sed diam nonummy nibh euismodem tincidunt ut laoreet dolore magna aliquam erat volutpat. Ut wisi enim ad minim veniam, quis nostrudzz exerci tation ullamcorper suscipit

The new wing will provide stack space for 30,000 titles and fifty more carrels.

enim ad minim veniam, quis nos-trud exerci tation ullamcorper sus-cipit lobortis nisl ut aliquip ex ea commodo consequat.

Duis autem vel eum iriuretam dolor in hendrerit in vulputate est velit esse molestie consequat, vel illum dolore eu feugiat nulla facil-isis at vero eros et accumsan et et iusto odio dignissim qui blandist praesent luptatum zzril delenissst augue duis dolore te feugait nulla facilisi.

Lorem ipsum dolor sit amet, consectetuer adipiscing elitttt, sed diam nonummy nibh euismod tin-cidunt ut laoreet dolore magna ali-quam erat volutpat. Ut wisi enim ad minim veniam, quis nostrudzz exerci tation ullamcorper suscipit

lobortis nisl ut aliquip ex ea com-modo consequat.

Duis autem vel eum iriure est dolor in hendrerit in vulputate et velit esse molestie consequat, vel illum dolore eu feugiat nulla num facilisis at vero eros et accumsan et iusto odio dignissim qui bland-it praesent luptatum zzril delenit augue duis dolore te feugait nulla facilisi.

Lorem ipsum dolor sit amet, consectetuer adipiscing elit, sed diam nonummy nibh euismodos tincidunt ut laoreet dolore magna aliquam erat volutpat. Vero eros et accumsan et iusto odio dignis-sim qui blandit praesent luptatum zzril delenit augue duis dolore te feugait nulla facilisi.

Traditional, Elegant

This newsletter works for a small college with a traditional look for its logo and print materials. A number of elements contribute to the classic look. It draws on the traditional three-column grid and several elements of nineteenth century typography. But the grid is interrupted by the visual and its offset caption, and the arrangement of the white space is quite modern. The college logo is screened back behind the title in the masthead and suggests the dignified elegance of monogrammed stationery.

Sabon has a delicate, old-fashioned look while the initial caps and the italic in the headline evoke nineteenth century typography. The italic "script" accents in the masthead complement the Futura and Sabon. The use of small caps and generous tracking on the heads give the Futura a classic feel.

Masthead: Sabon 70/50 and Sabon Italic (*The*) 36/50, tracking: +28, and (*Quarterly*) 60/50, tracking: +28
Logo: Sabon Italic 192 pt.
Heads: Futura Condensed 36 pt.
Captions: Futura Bold 11/18
Initial Caps: Sabon 36/18
Body: Sabon 11/18

Clean, Conservative

This clean, conservative newsletter will appeal both to new graduates with trendy tastes and to older alumni who want a more traditional look. The mix of Times Roman and Helvetica Black Condensed is a traditional one. However, the heads and captions are set small but black and generously leaded, creating some white space and making a more contemporary graphic statement. The subheads are stacked into short lines of flush left/rag right type to open up the page.

The three- or six-column grid offers opportunity for layout variety. Very short blocks of copy such as birth, marriage and death announcements, coming events, or a table of contents could occupy one or two small columns. Any copy more than a paragraph or two long will still need to be set over two of the six columns as shown here, however. Setting the captions in the black weight of a condensed face allows for readability in the narrow column. The word *News* is set in italic rather than continuing with the roman because the italic looks more active.

Masthead: Times Roman and Times Roman Italic, both 96 pt.
Heads: Helvetica Black Condensed caps 16/24
Captions: Helvetica Black Condensed 9/18
Body: Times 12/18

"Joe College" Look

Here, very generously leaded subheads and captions make a more graphic statement. A less static grid and an open column under the *A* in the masthead throw the layout off center. Bauer Bodoni and Futura Extra Bold Condensed offer strong contrast, especially with the leading of captions. The narrow column offers layout opportunities for graphic icons or marks run full strength or screened back.

The type in the masthead gives the newsletter a typical "rah-rah, Joe College" look intended to provoke nostalgia for their good old college days in alumni and parents of prospective freshmen. Futura Black has a sophisticated, stencil-style typeface. Screening back the *T* and the *U* gives the *A* a mark-like effect which could be carried throughout the newsletter as a graphic.

Masthead: Futura Black 144 pt. and Bauer Bodoni Condensed 96 pt.
Date: Futura Extra Bold Condensed 12 pt., manual letterspacing
Heads: Bauer Bodoni 31/38
Captions: Futura Extra Bold Condensed 11/36
Body: Bauer Bodoni 11/18

Fresh & Friendly

Goudy set in uppercase and lowercase gives this newsletter a homey touch to promote a family feeling. Although it is seldom used for newsletter design and therefore more visually interesting here, Goudy is quite readable and well suited to long blocks of text. The heavy weight and generous leading of the subheads are a contemporary graphic feature and give the newsletter a fresh, dynamic look.

Reversing the mast out of a solid color that will change with each issue offers an opportunity to differentiate at a glance between issues. This publication will stand out in a stack of mail; it won't look stodgy or boring.

Masthead: Goudy 120 pt., 36 pt. (*The*) and Futura Extra Bold 18pt., tracking: +39
Heads: Futura Extra Bold caps 16/38
Subhead: Futura Extra Bold Condensed 11/36
Captions: Futura Extra Bold Condensed 10/18
Body: Goudy 11/18

Dave Cundy

NCE UPON A TIME, IN 1980 TO BE EXACT,
DIGITAL TYPE WAS BORN. IN THOSE DAYS,
THERE WAS WIDESPREAD CRITICISM OF THAT
TECHNOLOGY, CRITICISM THAT THE JAGGED
LETTERFORMS OF THE EARLY DIGITAL TYPE-
SETTERS WEREN'T CRISP LIKE PHOTOTYPE
LETTERS. ALVIN EISENMAN, THEN DIRECTOR
OF STUDIES IN GRAPHIC DESIGN AT YALE,
DISAGREED, CALLING THE OBSOLESCENT
PHOTOTYPE "STERILE." HE PRAISED THE
PERSONALITY OF THE "JAGGIES," AND COM-
PARED DIGITAL LETTERFORMS TO LETTERPRESS
LETTERS THAT WERE NATURALLY DEFORMED
AND MISALIGNED BY THE COMPOSITION AND
PRINTING PROCESSES.

FIVE YEARS LATER, THE MACINTOSH WAS
BORN. AND WHILE CRITICS CITED THE CRUDITY
OF MAC DRAWING PROGRAMS, GRAPHIC DESIGNER
APRIL GREIMAN AND TYPE DESIGNER ZUZANA
LICKO SAW THE UNIQUE VISUAL LANGUAGE OF
THE BITMAP. BY WORKING WITH THIS LANGUAGE,
RATHER THAN BY TRYING TO EMULATE PRECEDING
TECHNOLOGIES, THESE DESIGNERS ACHIEVED
REMARKABLE, HIGHLY-ACCLAIMED RESULTS.

Idea Views

Design: John Waters, Dana Gonsalves
(logo by John Caruso)
© Waters Design Associates, Inc.
Size: 11" x 17"
Fonts: Mixed.
Primary Text Faces: Sabon, Futura in various weights
This newsletter for members of the International Design by
Electronics Association is produced on the Macintosh
using QuarkXPress and Adobe Illustrator. It takes a sophis-
ticated, graphic approach and employs some bit-mapped
display type as graphics.

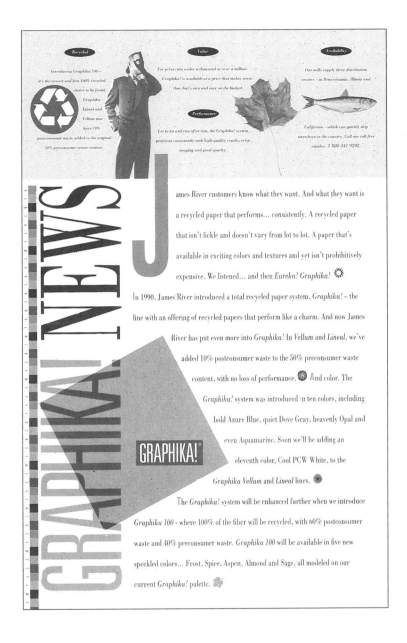

Graphika News

Design: Carol Bouyoucos, John Waters

© Waters Design Associates, Inc.

Size: 11" x 17"

Fonts: Univers and Bodoni

Designers and graphic arts professionals are the primary audience for this newsletter produced for the James River Paper Company. The use of lively visuals is appropriate to a piece that also acts as a marketing device. Generously leaded Bodoni text is graphic with its thicks and thins, and very legible, even on this issue's textured recycled fiber sheet.

LE DERNIER MOT
THE LAST WORD

Pour moi, le Canada c'est mon pays. J'y suis né et j'espère que nous serons, nous les Canadiens, assez adultes pour garder ce beau pays entier.

For me, Canada is my country. I was born here and I hope that we, we Canadians, will be adult enough to keep this beautiful country together.

LAURENT LAVOIE,
ROUYN-NORANDA, QUÉBEC

Panorama

Art Director: Diti Katona, John Pylypczak
Designer: Victoria Primicias
Illustrator: Jamie Bennet
Primary Font: Bembo

Panorama, a bimonthly bilingual publication for Noranda Group active and retired employees, tackles serious issues that affect the company and the country. Concrete, the design firm, uses a subdued palette of colors and typefaces with illustrations done in watercolor. The bold condensed sans serif primarily used for quotes, is softened with the use of color (turquoise).

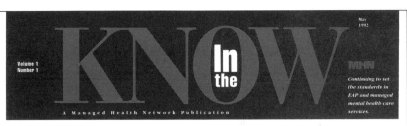

Searching for Solutions—Not Band-Aids

We're all aware of the heavy toll mental health and substance abuse problems take in the workplace. The issues reach far beyond the costs that result, and so must the solutions. Cost containment alone is not the answer — it's only a band-aid. Employers need to take a comprehensive, long-term approach to solve the problem — starting with examining the quality, appropriateness, and necessity of mental health and substance abuse treatment.

The Impact of Inappropriate Treatment

According to a study by the Michigan Health Care Education and Research Foundation and Blue Cross and Blue Shield of Michigan, nearly four out of 10 hospital stays for mental health and substance abuse treatment appear to be unnecessary. Moreover, 75% of inpatient admissions for substance abuse care were unnecessary. Inappropriate treatment is a widespread problem, and can adversely affect patient and payer alike.

The Effect on the Individual

Inpatient treatment has a dramatic, sometimes even traumatic, impact on an individual's life. When hospitalized, the individual gives up day-to-day control and is isolated from work, family and friends. Inappropriate inpatient treatment may even have negative effects. A survey of uncontrolled published studies of adult hospitalization (Canton and Cralnick, 1987) found that a majority of outcome studies showed that staying longer in a hospital does not increase the ability to function socially, and one study showed that the longer the hospitalization, the worse the social role-functioning became. Only one study showed a positive correlation between length of inpatient treatment and post-hospital functioning.

Hidden Costs

Several studies (Diehr et al., 1985; Shemo, 1986; Borus et al., 1985; McFarland et al.,

1985; Mumford et al., 1984) also show that untreated or inadequately treated psychiatrically ill or substance-abusing employees absorb an excessive amount of general medical services. In other words, the cost of inappropriate treatment can show up in medical insurance costs. According to

> **...nearly four out of 10 hospital stays for mental health and substance abuse treatment appear to be unnecessary.**

Mary Jane England, M.D., president of the Washington Business Group on Health, "Inappropriate and unnecessary treatment can even lead to an increase in disability and workers' compensation claims." Appropriate treatment reduces costs — both those that are direct and indirect.

Why Employers Need More Controls

Utilization of mental health and substance abuse services has nearly doubled in the past 10 years ("State mandates," October 1991). And, as the number of people seeking help increases, so does the problem of unnecessary and inappropriate mental health and sub-

stance abuse treatment. It's snowballing for several reasons.

Growing Acceptance

The stigma that once surrounded seeking help for mental health or substance abuse problems no longer exists. We are living in stressful times, and the general population realizes it's okay to need help.

Poor Treatment Selections

Consumers seeking help are often under mental distress and unaware of their treatment options, which can lead to irrational or inappropriate treatment selections. Providers, trying to prosper in a competitive marketplace, are using advertising to get people into treatment. With this combination, benefit users are making selections on where to go for help based on advertisements they see in the yellow pages and on television, or that they hear on the radio. Unfortunately, some of these mental health and substance abuse providers are often more concerned with making money than with ensuring that patients receive the most appropriate care.

Unethical Tactics

Recently, many treatment facilities have been under scrutiny for their unethical tactics. Several states have launched investigations into questionable methods of patient recruitment used by some psychiatric hospitals. Allegations include illegal kickbacks, billing for unnecessary services, and

billing for services that were not provided. A recent L.A. Times cover story revealed that, "Across the country, from New Jersey to Texas to California, patients contend that private psychiatric hospitals have been misdiagnosing them and holding them against their will to milk their insurance" (Moffat, February 3, 1992). Their employers must contend with employees being lassoed in by some hospitals and treatment centers, putting the individual's well-being in jeopardy and using up benefits unnecessarily.

Restrictive Benefit Designs Foster Inappropriate Treatment

Traditional insurers remain biased against alternative methods of treatment. They will pay for a 28-day inpatient stay, but won't pay for alternative programs that use equally effective, yet less expensive methods of treatment. A far-reaching literature survey (Melton, 1986) concludes, "Every study that has compared the efficacy of treatment for clients randomly assigned to inpatient or alternative services has found the latter

Medical Necessity Tests for Outpatient Treatment

A lesson should be learned from the evolution in medical and surgical cost management — with focus on decreasing unnecessary inpatient utilization, outpatient abuses increased. Managed mental health benefits must avoid this trend by managing outpatient care even more closely. Employers looking for ways to ensure appropriate treatment and control the unnecessary use of benefits should not overlook the importance of a truly sophisticated outpatient utilization management program.

Managed Health Network designed an effective, scientifically based method of determining the necessity of, duration of and reimbursement for outpatient treatment. Derogatis' Brief Symptom Inventory (BSI) allows us to identify, at the time of initial assessment, individuals who are experiencing primarily problems of living (such as financial troubles or marital difficulties), but do not have a true mental health or substance abuse problem. While these individuals may choose to purchase counseling or psychotherapy out of their discretionary income, it is not appropriate for that service to be paid for out of their medical insurance since it is not a medically necessary service.

Still, these problems of living do exist. Without help, employees' productivity and job performance can suffer. Employee assistance programs offer a solution. They're designed to help employees with a wide range of problems including problems of living. Many of these problems can be successfully resolved through the EAP.

In the KNOW

Designer: Angie Boothroyd
Art Director: Stan Evenson
Client: Managed Health Network
Size: 11" x 17"
Primary Font: Bodoni (Mast, display), Garamond condensed

In the KNOW, a Managed Health Network publication, presents news for the health care industry in a sophisticated multi-column treatment reminiscent of magazine layout. Sidebars, heavy rules, bold graphics, and callouts set in a black condensed sans serif provide relief from the long text.

Nine years ago this month, former WFAE staffer Fiona Ritchie first broadcast *The Thistle & Shamrock* nationwide. Today, more than 250 public radio stations carry this fascinating mix of Celtic music. Join WFAE on Saturday, June 6th at 8 pm, as Fiona presents music from her first playlist, including The Bothy Band, Christine Primrose, and The Tannahill Weavers.

A LITTLE MONEY, A LOT OF INSURANCE

In April, Dan Hoffman joined WFAE as development associate for corporate underwriting. How does underwriting work? Read on.

WFAE listeners regularly hear, "This hour of news/music is made possible in part by...." A company's name and message follow. That is an underwriting credit. Many people associate underwriting with the insurance industry, and while the term applies to both businesses — more on that later — it has special meaning to public radio.

Public radio exists because of listeners who decide to give money to help offset operating costs. Individual donors are called station subscribers.

A company which makes a contribution becomes an underwriter. Businesses underwrite WFAE's news or music for several reasons. One is simply to be a good corporate citizen. Contributing companies also understand the marketing value of reaching WFAE's audience.

WFAE's loyal listeners are well-educated, mid- to upper level income, and generally occupy positions of responsibility in their work. They are a desirable demographic target for many companies.

Businesses can reach these companies because we give on-air credits to underwriters in return for their support. These 12-second announcements are not commercials; WFAE is by law a non-commercial station. But underwriters may use on-air credits to talk about their products or services, as long as credit language meets public radio guidelines.

How is public radio underwriting related to the insurance variety? One definition of underwriting is "to guarantee financial support of." In that sense, our underwriters help insure the future of WFAE. They also insure themselves access to a worthwhile market.

Interested in exploring underwriting? Call me or Tony Reevy at 549-WFAE. We all can use more insurance. •
— Dan Hoffman

Dan Hoffman starts to sort through his new life at WFAE.

PAGE 2

THROUGH PROGRAMMING, PROMOTIONS, AND ACTION, WFAE EXPRESSES ENVIRONMENTAL COMMITMENT

WFAE listeners are passionately concerned about the environment, judging from comments we receive. Here's how we've responded.

Programming

Along with extensive environmental coverage on *Morning Edition, All Things Considered* and *The Carolina Chronicle*, 90.7 FM broadcasts *Living On Earth*, NPR's newsmagazine devoted exclusively to the environment, every Sunday at 7:30 am.

The newsmagazine, hosted by Steve Curwood, begins with a five-minute roundup of global and national environmental news. An in-depth series of reports on a single issue follows.

Topics have included how northeastern U.S. and Canadian forests survive acid rain; the state of Alaskan and New England fishing waters; solar, renewable, and fossil fuels; and the politics of lead poisoning. Future editions will cover Presidential candidates' specific environmental plans.

Promotions

WFAE co-sponsors several environmental projects each year. Through a media co-sponsorship, we help productive organizations get the word out about what they're doing and what they need.

In the spring, WFAE worked closely with the Charlotte-Mecklenburg Earth Coalition, creators of Earth Day. The station aired numerous announcements about Earth Day and broadcast live, on-location reports throughout the day.

Talking The Talk, and Walking The Walk

WFAE staffers recycle — maybe a little compulsively. Our program includes:

* reusing audio tape as many times as possible.
* recycling parts from old equipment.
* finding new uses for old equipment.
* receiving Associated Press newswire stories on computer, rather than in print, to save paper.

Recycling can have a minor drawback, station recycling guru Mark Perzel admits. "We've got enough scrap paper for phone messages," he says, "to last until the next millennium." •

WFAE, CAROWINDS PRESENT BLUES AND JAZZ FESTIVAL

Start with Spyro Gyra, Keiko Matsui, and other top artists in jazz and blues. Add a barbecue cook-off, an ethnic food fair, and an arts and crafts exhibition, and you've got a party you can hear, taste, and see.

Spend an entertaining weekend with other WFAE listeners on Saturday, May 30th and Sunday, May 31st, when WFAE and Carowinds host The Paladium's Blues and Jazz Festival.

Fans of WFAE's *The Blues Show* should stop by on Saturday, when the blues line-up will include Albert King and The Nighthawks.

Jazz takes over on Sunday, with music from Spyro Gyra, Keiko Matsui, Kilauea, Flight 108, Beth Chorneau, Side One and Faction. Tickets are $10 per day for a reserved festival seat, or $21.95 for a one-day reserved festival seat and Carowinds admission. Call the Paladium Box Office, 588-2606, ext. 2226, for details. •

Keiko Matsui

Spyro Gyra

ECOFILE

An office of 60 employees produces a ton of paper a month. If that ton was recycled, we could save enough energy to power an average home for six months!

WFAE Notes

Art Direction and Design: Robin Poosikan Kasparian
Client: WFAE
Size: 8 ½" x 11"
Fonts: Caslon 540 and Franklin Gothic Heavy
Illustration: M.L. Hedin
Photography: Diane Davis
Writer/Editor: Andrea Cooper

Each issue of this lively, radio station newsletter is printed in two colors other than black. Cartoons, clip art, graphics obtained from a variety of sources and display type add variety to text laid out with a four-column grid.

Strategic Plan

The ink is now dry on The St. Catharines General Hospital's road map for the future, a map that includes plans for a new trauma unit, better services for the elderly, and the establishment of a women's health care centre.

Called Framework for the Future, the strategic plan – a product of six months worth of meetings, weekend retreats and consultations with the hospital's staff and administration – was approved last fall by the Board of Governors.

Hospital president, Bob McCann, notes many of the concepts embodied in the plan merely confirm the directions the hospital was taking, following "the natural flow of progression."

That progression, geared toward steering St. Catharines' largest hospital into the 21st century, is spelled out in four areas of the 22-page plan; trauma services, the general vs. specialized hospital debate, and regional health services.

TRAUMA SERVICES
Slated for development in the next two or three years is a trauma unit that will allow The General to handle serious emergency cases. This will relieve the burden shouldered by Hamilton and Toronto hospitals, where many Niagara trauma patients are now transferred.

Also planned are more trauma nurses to serve the centre, as well as the purchase of new equipment with the specialized demands of trauma medicine.

GERIATRIC SERVICES
To keep pace with the health needs of St. Catharines' burgeoning elderly population, The General intends to boost services geared towards geriatric care, while streamlining its chronic care facilities.

A geriatrician should be hired within the year to head a team that will implement The General's new geriatric programs, including establishing a rapid-response team to diagnose patients, and new psychogeriatric services based on out-patient visits.

While the hospital has completed its planned 36-bed chronic care unit, all other patients with long-term needs will be moved to other facilities or integrated back into the community – a move in line with Ministry of Health directives.

A GENERAL OR SPECIALIZED HOSPITAL?
Put simply, The General will stay general, at least through the 1990's. We will continue to provide patients with the varied services that have traditionally been our hallmark.

But we'll also continue to develop speciality services to support the general services already being provided. Aside from the previously mentioned trauma unit, some of those speciality referral services include:
● vascular surgery, with an increased diagnostic component
● obstetrical services, including neonatal intensive care and midwifery

● a women's health centre and sexual assault centre
● increased out-patient and day-care facilities
● enhanced psychiatric programs, including psychogeriatrics
● an upgrading and extension of diagnostic services

THE GENERAL AS A REGIONAL HEALTH CENTRE
The future of the hospital as a Regional Acute Care Centre is solid, with the strategic plan calling for the retention and enhancement of several services provided to Niagara residents exclusively by The General. They include diagnostic and imaging services, psychogeriatric care and assessment, thoracic and vascular surgery, as well as maternal and child care.

The intricacies of future regional development haven't been worked out yet, pending discussion with other health centres and agencies, and the completion of an impact study.

Flower Ladies

Run for the General

Check your calendar and warm up your running shoes because the Sixth Annual Run for The General is set for Sunday, June 14, 1992 starting at 10:00 a.m. Like last year, the Run for The General will cover a four mile circuit along Vansickle Road to Pelham Road, First Street Louth, and along St. Paul Street West. The start-finish line is at Club Roma on Vansickle Road.

"Taking the race out of the city centre to the country roadways has resulted in an almost hassle-free course," explains race coordinator Mike Coletti, a.k.a. the hospital's Risk Manager.

"It's a safer race course mostly because of the light vehicular traffic in the area," says Mike. "With the new race location, we also were able to host a barbecue. We'll be doing the same for 1992. All participants will receive free drinks, hamburgs or hot dogs."

Spectators can purchase their food and are more than welcome to pack up a picnic and bring out the kids.

Mike notes that while walkers have historically been well represented, there were fewer at last year's event. "We're planning to improve recognition of the race walkers through some special awards and trophies." He adds that walkers and runners will also receive a snazzy, commemorative race T-shirt - "a real collector's item".

A special challenge is also being issued to all hospital employees to compete for The General's Team Trophy. The race has been a significant fundraiser. In the past five years more than $43,800 has been raised through pledges and race donations. There's been a lot of spirit and support behind the Run for The General, and we hope the tradition continues for a long time to come.

For more information on the Run for The General, call Public Relations at Ext. 4353 or Mike Coletti at Ext. 4638.

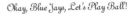

Okay, Blue Jays, Let's Play Ball!

The familiar chant of the ever-popular Toronto Blue Jays Baseball Club echoed through the corridors of Community 6 on January 22nd when six of Hogtown's 1991 American League semi-finalists rolled into The General's Paediatric Unit.

The Blue Jays Second Baseman Roberto Alomar, In-fielder Pat Tabler, Pitcher Duane Ward, Out-fielder Devon White, Out-fielder Candy Maldonato, along with Pitching Coach Galen Cisco were at the hospital thanks to the generous hospitality of The St. Catharines Blue Jays and Labatt's Breweries.

"It's great to see the kids," remarked Devon White. "Big and small! When we get away from the game and do these visits, it really puts things back into perspective. This is what it's all about."

Five year old Jessica had no problem letting eight year veteran Pat Tabler know who her favourite player was. "Jim Kelly - don't ya know. He plays for the Bills."

The players signed autographs, passed out "Baseball Mania" board games, and snapped photos with the children, their parents and a cross-section of hospital staff.

Christine Clark, our Co-ordinator of Public Relations, notes that "The Jays visit could be one of the best kept secrets we've experienced. While obviously there are a lot of disappointed die-hard fans, I think everyone can appreciate that we were obliged to respect the players' wishes and maintain a reasonable level of traffic on the nursing unit."

Paediatric patient, Mathew Wortel, got the thrill of a lifetime when members of the Toronto Blue Jays Baseball Club visited on January 22nd!

Continuing Care Unit Update

Formerly known as the Chronic Care Unit, the Continuing Care Unit is a 13,120 square foot facility located on the adjoining second floors of the Moore and McSloy Wings. The area is accessible by the Moore Elevator, Norris 2 and 3 stairwells.

● The Continuing Care Unit was reopened in early April 1992 following an extensive $2.3 million redevelopment.
● The Continuing Care Unit will accommodate 36 long term care patients.

For the first time, the Continuing Care Unit will bring the specialized services of occupational therapy, recreational therapy and physiotherapy for long term care together into one area.
● New features include wheelchair accessible washroom facilities in each patient room; a Thune whirlpool tub which incorporates a stretcher to lift patients in and out of the tub; shower facilities; a family room; washer and dryer for patient laundry; dining room; and a daily living room equipped with a wheelchair accessible kitchen. A solarium installed in the dining area as a unique architectural feature.
● Two-thirds of the funding for the redevelopment of the Continuing Care Unit comes from the taxpayers of Ontario through the Ministry of Health, with the additional funds raised through donors to The St. Catharine General Hospital Foundation.
● "We've always had quality of patient care, but because of the improved facilities, we'll be able to improve quality of life for our patients."
Patty Berard, Occupational Therapy
● "Finally, a dream come true! We've been looking forward to this for so many years."
Lee Watson, Discharge Planner
● "All members of the Continuing Care Unit multi-disciplinary group will now be able to really work together as a Team."
Evelyn Romanek, Social Work
● "Oh, I think everyone has anxiously waited for the new chronic unit. I graduated from nursing in 1958. I worked Moore One through Moore 3 in the 1960's. I'm looking forward to concluding my career on a higher note by retiring next year as an R.N. from the Continuing Care Unit."
Isabel Barkwell, R.N.
● "I've always enjoyed working with the patients on the chronic floors. With the new unit, there'll be a lot of changes, but one thing that will remain the same is, like old times, we'll all be just one of the family."
Christine McNeil, Housekeeping
● "The previous facility was very outdated. Finally, we have a facility that can more than adequately meet our patients' needs."
Donna Malone, Nurse Manager, Mills 2 Floor

The News in General

Art Director: John Pylypczak, Diti Katona
Client: St. Catherine's General Hospital
Designer: Victoria Primicias
Size: 11" x 17"
Font: Centaur
St. Catherine's General Hospital newsletter takes a somewhat nostalgic approach with human interest stories while presenting editorial from the hospital's perspective about health care issues. The photos are large. Initial caps and decorative typographic flourishes work with the warm second color and the cream-colored stock.

SMU Meadows Newsletter

Designer: Scott Paramski
Client: SMU
© 1992 Peterson & Company
Fonts: Bodoni and various

Meadows is published by Meadows School of the Arts at
Southern Methodist University. It is dynamic and graphic
in its use of large, bold type, smaller text, and generous use
of white space. The halftones are often outlined and used
quite large for balance.

SERVICE

NOBODY PROVIDES BETTER SERVICE NOBODY

Service personal the wishes of every is taking a interest in each and customer. It's taking that extra effort to anticipate the needs of the customer and providing them with whatever they need. It's being friendly, helpful and willing to assist. We want our customers to leave our Tradewell, PriceSetter or Prairie Markets convinced they got the most for their food dollar and that they were served by people who were happy to serve them and ready to serve them again. We'll do whatever it takes to ensure our customers have the finest shopping experience available. We want them to tell their friends and neighbors about the people of the Tradewell Group, our dedication to service, our friendliness and our desire to please. Nobody will provide better service then we do. Nobody!

Market Report
Volume 1, Number 1

Fall 1986
Tradewell Stores Group

Editor's Note

Welcome to the first issue of *Market Report*, the monthly newsletter for the employees of the Tradewell Group. *Market Report* will be coming to you each month filled with news of your company, its activities and people as well as corporate philosophies and practices. We think it will be a valuable asset in helping you understand the new direction we are taking in an effort to provide the very best service we can offer.

The first issue will be dedicated to the management and corporate philosophies of Tom Stewart and his new management team - many of whom you may already know.

The next several months will be very exciting for all of us associated with the new Tradewell Group as we work to make our stores the very best in the Pacific Northwest. We're convinced we can accomplish this goal. Together we will lead the retail grocery industry through example and demonstrate we are indeed "On the Move Again."

This issue is devoted to a topic which will be the foundation of the new Tradewell Group - **Service.** The companies of Services Group of America have each succeeded by providing the very best service to their customers possible, no matter what industry they operate in. And, they make money doing it.

We're going to do the same. Each and every one of our customers will receive the best service available in the grocery business today!

We're here to serve you as much as you're here to serve the customer. We want to hear from you. Drop us a line and tell us what you think about *Market Report.* We want this publication to be useful to you and your input will help us accomplish that. So read on - we think you'll like what you see.

Bill Rozier
Editor

Store Directors to Meet Every Two Weeks. Common Language and Team Work is the Key.

All Tradewell Group Store Directors have begun a bi-weekly meeting program in which everyone comes together for an evening to discuss operating priorities and problems similar to each store. The meetings are headed by President Tom Stewart and feature reports by the various operating divisions.

"We are completely restructuring and rethinking the way we approach the retail grocery business," explains Stewart. "If the Renton store is experiencing problems getting correct invoices from a supplier, it's a good bet someone else in the system is also having problems."

"These meetings are intended to establish a working communication between all stores in the system. If Renton has a problem, let's put 37 heads together and find the right answer."

The meetings are called to order by Stewart with a brief update on company performance and progress. Division vice presidents all

Continued on back page.

Service

Design: Hornall Anderson
Client: Tradewell
This very visual newsletter for employees of Tradewell and PriceSetter Stores serves to spread company news and share the corporate philosophy. The colorful, graphic approach and stencil display type are appropriate for a newsletter for a retail client.

esign

&

ABCDEFG

TYP

12345

M

Ads

ere, we will look at ads that rely heavily on text—and therefore type—to sell products. Where the art or photo says it all, use it large; choose an unobtrusive face for the tag line or address and phone number. Ideally, when designing an ad, you are working in conjunction with a copywriter, or at least have input on copy. A single message, repeated and reinforced with appropriate typography, is always more effective than a mixed signal.

How do you tell the audience that this ad is for them? Since they're being bombarded with advertising, they'll consider the ad that seems to understand who they are. Market research can define the target audience and the emotion(s) the ad should evoke. What is the audience looking for in the product or service? Is it credibility, and authority (for a lawyer or accountant), security (for a bank or insurance company), or romance (for a restaurant or travel agent)?

Finally, where will they see the ad? A fractional ad in a newspaper will float in a sea of text and other graphics. To be noticed, it will need to stand apart. A full-page ad in a trade or targeted publication has the attention of the target audience, and no competition on the page. The mood or message can be softer or more straightforward.

Type Considerations

Unless you're designing an advertorial, where editorial rules apply, ad typography is generally trendier, and it is acceptable to use faces with more character, in order to support the advertising mood or message.

Unless you stop them, the audience will flip past your ad. It's important to attract attention and lead the viewer around the information. You can use type size and weight to guide the eye from the headline to a product shot, then on to the caption if there is one, down to the logo, back to bold subheads, then into body copy. If the ad is to enhance the company's image (as is the case with some industrial ads), it may have no body copy. A direct response ad will have more support copy and order information. The reader should not be confused by the image or discouraged from ordering by being forced to hunt for the toll-free number.

Specializing in Women's Health Care

Lorem ipsum dolor sit amet, consectetuer adipiscing elit, sed diam nonummy nibh euismod tincidunt ut laoreet dolore magna aliquam erat volutpat. Ut wisi enim ad minim veniam, quis nostrud exerci tation ullamcorper suscipit lobortis nisl ut aliquip ex ea commodo consequat. Duis autem vel eum iriure.

Wolor in hendrerit in vulputate velit esse molestie consequat, vel illum dolore eu feugiat nulla facilisis at vero eros et accumsan et

iusto odio dignissim qui blandit praesent luptatum zzril delenit augue duis dolore te feugait nulla facilisi. Lorem ipsum dolor sit amet, consectetuer adipiscing elit, sed diam nonummy nibh

Ut wisi enim ad minim veniam, quis nostrud exerci tation ullamcorper suscipit lobortis nisl ut aliquip ex ea commodo consequat. Duis autem vel eum iriure dolor in hendrerit in vulputate velit esse molestie consequat, vel illum dolore eu feugiat nulla

THE MIDTOWN CLINIC

Your Child's Nutritional Needs Are as Simple as...

Aorem ipsum dolor sit amet, consecteteur adopiscing elit, sed diam nonummy nibh euis adipiscing elit, sed diam nonummy nibh. Lorem ipsum sit amet, consecteteur adipising elit, nonum nonummm doloreus.

MidTown Pediatric Center

Bed diam nonummy nibh euis adipiscing elit, sed diam nonummy nibh. Lorem ipsum sit amet, consecteteut adipising elit, sed diam nonummy. sed diam nonummy nibh euis adipiscing elit, sed diam nonummy nibh. Lorem ipsum sit ametummy.

Consecteteur adopiscing elit, sed diam nonummy nibh euis adipiscing elit, sed diam nonummy nibh. Lorem ipsum sit amet, consecteteut adipising elit, sed diam nonummy. diam nonummy nibh euis adipiscing elib.

Credibility

This ad separates itself from the clamor of surrounding text and ads. The copy is an island in a calm sea of white space. And it has credibility. The presentation draws on techniques used for serious, digest-size publication design— long, centered headlines and a symmetrical, two-column grid surrounded by generous, equal-sized margins.

Optima has a classic, shimmering quality, especially in the all caps, widely tracked logotype. The hairline rule pulls your eye down to the logo if you're not inclined to read all of the text. The Sabon headline adds a "literary" credibility while the Optima lightens the impact of this text-heavy ad.

Headline: Sabon 70/70, horizontal scaling: 90%
Body: Optima 12/18, justified
Initial Caps: Sabon 24/18, horizontal scaling: 90%
Logotype: Optima caps 18/auto, tracking: +60 pt.

Comfortable, Reassuring

This ad has a look strongly reminiscent of children's story-books to project a comfortable, reassuring feeling. The Century headline and body type are staples of children's book design. The Bauer Bodoni Black initial caps resemble the type on alphabet blocks. Bold primary shapes interrupt the heavily leaded text for a bouncy effect.

Because this is an informational ad to promote the pediatric center by building a positive image of the center as a place that cares about parents and children, the logo occupies a small, less noticeable area of the ad. The heavily leaded text floats in a large pool of white space, but the eye is pulled to the heavy anchor of the logotype in the lower left corner.

Headline: Century 48/56
Body: Century 12/24
Initial Caps: Bauer Bodoni Black 60
Logotype: Futura Extra Bold 16/24

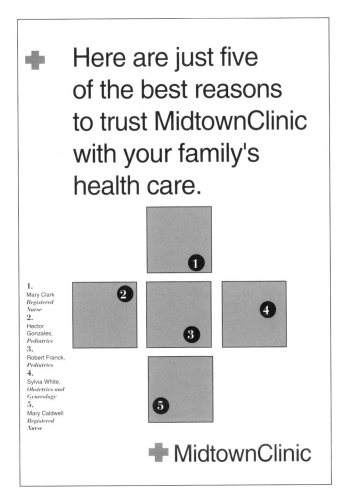

Clean, Corporate

A clean, corporate look like this can tie in with hospital signage or other elements of the whole identity program. Although the extra bold and black weights of Helvetica are most commonly used for headlines, this long, one-sentence headline would not be as legible in an extra bold weight. And this understated approach has a corporate, not a hard-sell look.

The simple, direct typography and layout draw attention to the pictures, close-ups of smiling health care workers, which are the sales message. Pictures always attract readers; the type and layout shouldn't compete. Helvetica is such a neutral typeface that it can be used extensively without overpowering the pictures. The Bauer Bodoni provides an attractive accent. Its set of numbers is quite pretty but delicate, so they were set off from the pictures by being reversed out of black circles.

Headline: Helvetica 40/48
Captions: Bauer Bodoni Italic 9/11 (numbers) and Helvetica 9/11
Numbers (on visuals): Bauer Bodoni Black 12/14
Logotype: Helvetica 36 pt.

Upbeat, Simple

This ad is aimed at an older audience who are most likely to need the center's services. The headline supports the invitation to be more active, and the copy is an upbeat story about the reader leading a normal life after surgery. The bold subhead and logo provide the necessary information.

This is not the place to tamper with legibility, since the audience may have difficulty reading. A heavily designed ad could be intimidating, so this ad achieves its effect with a simple graphic and the positioning of the copy and white space. The friendly italic serif and the flush left/rag right copy reinforce the left to right movement of the whole ad.

Headline: Palatino Italic 60/50
Subhead: Helvetica Black 10/18
Body: Palatino 12/18
Logotype: Helvetica Black 12/18

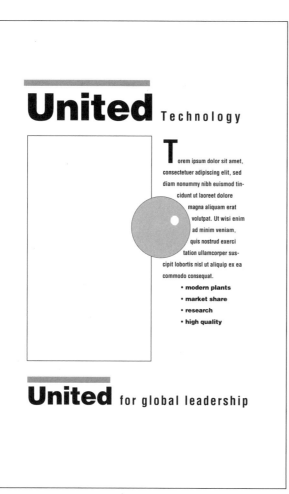

United Technology

Torem ipsum dolor sit amet, consectetuer adipiscing elit, sed diam nonummy nibh euismod tincidunt ut laoreet dolore magna aliquam erat volutpat. Ut wisi enim ad minim veniam, quis nostrud exerci tation ullamcorper suscipit lobortis nisl ut aliquip ex ea commodo consequat.

- **modern plants**
- **market share**
- **research**
- **high quality**

United for global leadership

Safety is our First Job.

Leugiat nulla facilisis at vero eros et accumsan et iusto odio dignissim qui blandit praesent luptatum zzril delenit augue duis dolore te feugait nulla facilisi. Lorem ipsum dolor sit amet, consectetuer adipiscing elit, sed diam nonummy nibh euismod tincidunt ut laoreet dolore magna aliquam erat volutpat.

Ut wisi enim ad minim veniam, quis nostrud exerci tation ullamcorper suscipit lobortis nisl ut aliquip ex ea commodo consequat. Duis autem vel eum iriure dolor in hendrerit in vulputate velit esse molestie consequat, vel illum dolore eu feugiat nulla facilisis at vero eros et accumsan et iusto odio dignissim qui blandit praesent luptatum zzril delenit augue duis dolore te feugait nulla facilisi

Leugiat nulla facilisis at vero eros et accumsan et iusto odio dignissim qui blandit praesent luptatum zzril delenit augue duis dolore te feugait

CEO Ron Robb conducts a spot safety check.

nulla facilisi. Lorem ipsum dolor sit amet, consectetuer adipiscing elit, sed diam nonummy nibh euismod tincidunt ut laoreet dolore magna aliquam erat volutpat.

Ut wisi enim ad minim veniam, quis nostrud exerci tation ullamcorper suscipit lobortis nisl ut aliquip ex ea

United

for a safer workplace.

commodo consequat. Duis autem vel eum iriure dolor in hendrerit in vulputate velit esse molestie consequat, vel illum dolore eu feugiat nulla facilisis at vero eros et accumsan et iusto odio dignissim qui blandit praesent luptatum zzril delenit augue duis dolore te feugait nulla facilisi

Leugiat nulla facilisis at vero eros et accumsan et iusto odio dignissim qui blandit praesent luptatum zzril delenit augue duis dolore te feugait nulla facilisi. Lorem ipsum dolor sit amet, consectetuer adipiscing elit, sed diam nonummy nibh euismod tincidunt ut laoreet dolore magna aliquam erat volutpat.

Ut wisi enim ad minim veniam, quis nostrud exerci tation ullamcorper suscipit lobortis nisl ut aliquip ex ea commodo consequat. Duis autem vel eum iriure dolor in hendrerit in vulputate velit esse molestie consequatfn et iusto odiogait nulla

---

Clean, Contemporary

This ad, typical of the image ads large industrial corporations place in trade magazines, is put together to present a strong, single image to the busy, casual reader. A business person flipping through the magazine sees a dramatic photo, the company logo, and the clean, contemporary typography of the minimal copy. A generously tracked Helvetica Bold Condensed in the headline and logo has a contemporary look that fits this approach.

For a unified typographic look, only Helvetica Black and Helvetica Bold Condensed are used for the whole ad. The bulleted benefits or services of the company appear in the heavier weight to ensure that they catch the skimmer's eye even if the rest of the copy isn't read.

Headline: Helvetica Black 72 pt., and Helvetica Bold Condensed 24/auto, tracking: +22
Body: Helvetica Bold Condensed 12/22
Bulleted Copy: Helvetica Black 12/22
Logotype: Helvetica Black 48 pt., and Helvetica Bold Condensed 24 pt., tracking: +22

Serious, Journalistic

This ad borrows from straightforward magazine design and is meant to resemble an editorial. This spare design has only a photo of the president or spokesperson for a graphic element—no rules or decorative borders. This styling also works well for a testimonial ad, where the only graphic would be a shot of the satisfied consumer or the wonderful product.

The serious-sounding copy and headline are the key elements, so it is important not to use a frivolous typeface. Times was chosen here because of its long association with journalism. Futura is the choice here because it has a very graphic and slightly geometric quality. The layout and the type work to ensure that skimming readers will at least notice the headline, the photo and its caption, and the logo and slogan.

Head: Times 90/80, horizontal scaling: 95%
Body: Times 12/16
Captions: Futura Extra Bold Condensed 12/16
Logotype: Futura Extra Bold Condensed 36 pt., 19 pts. baseline to baseline to the first line of the slogan
Slogan: Futura Extra Bold Condensed 18/20

"Advertorial"

This image ad targets the general consumer rather than a business. It is almost an advertorial. The Century body type gives the ad a book-like quality, as do other book elements such as the double border and the rules separating columns of type. This projects a serious, editorial feeling that enhances the credibility of the message. It is important that the company logo be small and part of a message. It would contradict the approach to grandstand.

The two callouts have intriguing quotes from experts to encourage readers to explore the copy. The ad is heavily illustrated with long, informative captions set in dark Helvetica Bold Condensed for the same reason. Even if they don't read all of the text of this ad, many "readers" will still absorb the impression that this company cared enough to research and tell its story.

Head: Century 95 pt., horizontal scaling: 95%, tight letterspacing
Body: Century 12/20
Captions: Helvetica Black Condensed 11/16, centered
Callouts: Helvetica Black Condensed 11/16, centered

A LIVING WILL FOR YOUR PEACE OF MIND

Spare your loved ones pain. Consectetuer adipiscing elit, sed diam nonummy nibh euismod tincidunt ut laoreet dolore magna aliquam erat volutpat. Ut wisi enim ad minim veniam, quis nostrud exerci. Ut wisi enim ad minim veniam, quis.
Medical choices. Duis autem vel eum iriure dolor in hendrerit in vulputate velit esse molestie consequat, vel illum dolore eu feugiat nulla facilisis at vero eros et accumsan et iusto odio dignissim qui blandit praesent luptatum zzril delenit augue duis dolore te feugait nulla facilisi. Lorem ipsum dolor sit amet, consectetuer adipiscing elit, sed diam nonummy nibh euismod tincidunt ut laoreet dolore magna aliquam erat volutpat.
Let us help you make plans now. Duis autem vel eum iriure dolor in hendrerit in vulputate velit esse molestie consequat, vel illum dolore eu feugiat nulla facilisis at vero eros et accumsan et iusto odio dignissim qui blandit praesent luptatum zzril delenit augue duis dolore te feugait nulla facilisi. Lorem ipsum dolor sit amet.

BAILEY, YOUNG & BARSTOW
ATTORNEYS AT LAW

A LIVING WILL *for Your Peace of Mind*

Spare your loved ones pain. Consectetuer adipiscing elit, sed diam nonummy nibh euismod tincidunt ut laoreet dolore magna aliquam erat volutpat. Ut wisi enim ad minim veniam, quis nostrud exerci tation ullamcorper suscipit lobortis nisl ut aliquip ex ea commodo.
Let medical personnel know your wishes. Ut wisi enim ad minim veniam, quis nostrud exerci tation ullamcorper suscipit lobortis nisl ut aliquip ex ea commodo consequat.consectetuer adipiscing elit, sed diam nonummy nibh euismod tincidunt ut laoreet dolore magna aliquam erat volutpat. Ut wisi enim ad minim veniam, quis nostrud exerci tation ullamcorper suscipit lobortis nisl ut aliquip ex ea commodo consequat..
Let us help you make plans now. Consec tetuer adipiscing elit, sed diam nonummy nibh euismod tincidunt ut laoreet dolore magna aliquam erat volutpat. Ut wisi enim ad minim veniam, quis nostrud exerci tation ullamcorper suscipit lobortis nisl ut aliquip ex ea commodo. Ut wisi enim ad minim veniam, quis nostrud exercilation.

BAILEY, YOUNG & BARSTOW
Attorneys at Law

Timeless, Dignified

The head, text and logotype of this ad form a pillar shape to evoke classic monuments and by implication eternity and timeless quality. The subheads are run in so they don't interrupt the column shape.

Slightly condensed Goudy in small caps has a timeless, formal quality, and is reminiscent of text etched in stone. Because Goudy is a rather delicate face, Optima, which is often described as a "serifless" rather than a sans serif, has been used for the subheads. There is just enough contrast, combined with the change in size, for the subheads to stand out. A sans serif such as Helvetica, Universe or Futura would be far too obvious—even if set the same size as the body—for the subtle, understated typographic look.

Head: Goudy small caps 72/70, horizontal scaling: 90%
Body: Optima 10/16 justified
Subheads: Optima 14/16, run in
Logotype: Goudy small caps 18 pt., horizontal scaling: 90%, and Optima small caps 14 pt.

Restrained, Formal

Another restrained approach, but one that is not as stylized as the other ad on this page. The generously pitched Optima also has a timeless, engraved look, but the Palatino Italic has a light, active look and reflects the typographic design of many church publications. Two justified columns with a wide border lends credibility through its formality.

Emphasis is handled softly and subtly throughout the piece. Subheads are run in with the text and distinguished only by a change in type size. The logotype is given emphasis by isolating it in a sea of white space, not weight. The Palatino Italic is not used often but provides a bright note to keep the ad's very simple, unified typography from becoming monotonous and dull.

Head: Optima small caps 64/70, tracking: +6, and Palatino Italic 60/70, horizontal scaling: 90%, tracking: -6
Subheads: Optima 14/16, run in
Body: Optima 10/16
Logotype: Optima small caps 30/30, horizontal scaling: 90%, tracking: -6, and Palatino Italic 24/30, horizontal scaling: 90%, tracking: -6

Considering Bankruptcy?

Free Consultation

Lorem ipsum dolor sit amet, Consectetuer adipiscing elit, sed diam nonummy nibh euismod tincidunt ut laoreet dolore magna aliquam erat volutpat. Ut wisi enim ad minim veniam, quis nostrud exerci tation ullamcorper suscipit lobortis nisl ut aliquip ex ea commodo consequat.

Duis autem vel eum iriure dolor in hendrerit in vulputate velit esse molestie consequat, vel illum dolore eu feugiat nulla facilisis at vero eros et accumsan et iusto odio dignissim qui blandit praesent luptatum zzril delenit augue duis dolore te feugait nulla facilisi. Lorem ipsum dolor sit amet, consectetuer adipiscing elit, sed diam nonummy nibh euismod tincidunt ut laoreet dolore magna aliquam erat volutpat.

Ut wisi enim ad minim veniam, quis nostrud exerci tation ullamcorper suscipit lobortis nisl ut aliquip ex ea commodo consequat. Duis autem vel eum iriure dolor in hendrerit in vulputate velit esse molestie consequat, vel illum dolore eu feugiat nulla facilisis at vero eros et accumsan et iusto odio dignissim qui blandit praesent luptatum zzril delenit augue duis dolore te feugait nulla facilisi.

BAILEY, YOUNG & BARSTOW
ATTORNEYS AT LAW

Considering Bankruptcy?

Lorem ipsum dolor sit amet, Consectetuer adipiscing elit, sed diam nonummy nibh euismod tincidunt ut laoreet dolore magna aliquam erat volutpat. Ut wisi enim ad minim veniam, quis nostrud exerci tation ullamcorper suscipit lobortis nisl ut aliquip ex ea commodo ex nisa labortis consequat.

Duis autem vel eum iriure dolor in hendrerit in vulputate velit esse molestie consequat, vel illum dolore eu feugiat nulla facilisis at vero eros et accumsan et iusto odio dignissim qui blandit praesent luptatum zzril delenit augue duis dolore te feugait nulla facilisi. Lorem ipsum dolor sit amet, consectetuer adipiscing elit, sed diam nonummy nibh euismod tincidunt ut laoreet dolore magna aliquam erat volutpat.

Ut wisi enim ad minim veniam, quis nostrud exerci tation ullamcorper suscipit lobortis nisl ut aliquip ex ea commodo consequat.

BAILEY, YOUNG & BARSTOW
Attorneys at Law

Bold, Direct

This very direct ad mimics the classifieds with a short, bold headline. The body copy is more elegant and restrained than that of a typical classified ad and is set off from the border with a generous amount of white space. If the copy didn't offset the bold headline, the ad would appear garish and cheap, rather than appearing direct but professional.

Helvetica Condensed fits well into ads like this where space is at a premium, and this black weight makes a strong, forceful statement. The justified copy is in Bauer Bodoni, a face that imparts an air of elegance to any type design. Since Bodoni can be difficult to read, make sure the printer can hold the thin letters of Bodoni if your text is too long to appear in 12-point type.

Head: Helvetica Black Condensed 72/76
Subhead: Bauer Bodoni Italic 36/70, horizontal scaling: 90%
Body: Bauer Bodoni 12/18, justified
Logotype: Bauer Bodoni small caps 26/30, horizontal scaling: 90%, and Helvetica Black Condensed 18/30, tracking: +20

Hit the Highlights

Here the benefit, the free consultation, is set off as a violator in a standard retail convention. It is meant to also conjure up images of "overdue" stamps on bills. Tightly tracked, centered Times Roman is a standard for ad headlines. Although the headline occupies only a small portion of the ad, the major change in type size and the large amount of white space around it attract your eye. If you read only the extra bold copy as you move past the ad, you will get the key points: "FREE consultation" and the firm's name.

Head: Times Roman 80/76, horizontal scaling: 90%, tracking: -3
Violator: Futura Extra Bold 60 pt., 30 pts. baseline to baseline to the second line, and Futura Extra Bold 24/30
Body: Times Roman 12/18, justified
Logotype: Futura Condensed Extra Bold small caps 26/30 and Times Roman Italic 18/30

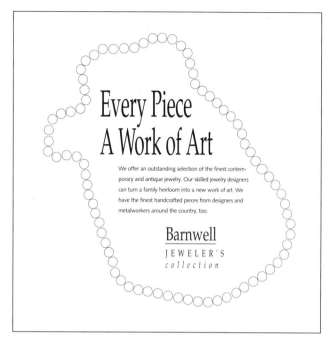

Image of Artistry

There's usually not much copy in an ad like this where the key thing is to project an image. The space isn't filled wall-to-wall with copy. Instead the emphasis is on the "artistry" implied in the headline, and the careful placement—no crowding—of the elements. The string of pearls creates a soft border.

Palatino is a pretty face with a calligraphic quality well-suited to the upscale image of this ad. It's also very versatile as the logo demonstrates. Syntax is an excellent complement to the Palatino here because it is one of the few sans serif typefaces that attempt to capture the spontaneous, rhythmic look of calligraphy. Syntax body copy looks better when set with generous leading, although it doesn't always have to have as much as shown here.

Dimensions: 7 ¼" x 7 ¼"
Head: Palatino 72/72, horizontal scaling: 50%
Body: Syntax 11/20
Logotype: Palatino u/lc 36 pt., horizontal scaling: 70%, Palatino all caps 18/21, horizontal scaling: 70%, manual letterspacing, and Palatino Italic 18/21, horizontal scaling: 70%

Classic, Elegant

The antique "frame" with a "mat" of white space sets off this classic ad. The copy is set in the tradition of nineteenth century books with an initial cap. The inset photo would usually be a close-up shot of a ring or brooch.

Sabon is a classic, elegant typeface that gives a feeling of traditional quality to the logo. It has been picked up for the headline, where the *T* and the *W* especially look as if they have just been lifted from a nineteenth century book. Optima is a graceful complement to the Old World look of the Sabon. Optima benefits from generous line spacing as it has been given here.

Dimensions: 7 ¼" x 7 ¼"
Head: Sabon small caps 84/72, horizontal scaling: 50%
Initial Cap: Sabon 36 pt., horizontal scaling: 50%
Body: Optima 11/20
Logotype: Sabon 36 pt., horizontal scaling: 70%, Sabon, 14 pt., horizontal scaling: 70%, manual letterspacing, and Sabon Italic 14 pt., horizontal scaling: 70%, manual letterspacing

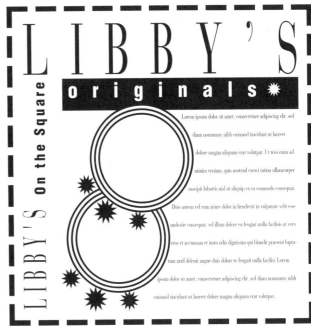

Bold, Primitive

Although this ad is copy heavy, the graphics catch your eye and set the mood. A bold, primitive look is achieved by "carving" Futura Extra Bold, and using high contrast graphics of the artist's work. The carved effect was created by "cutting" the type on screen with white rules of various lengths that were dragged over the letters in a somewhat random fashion.

The Futura Extra Bold is the dominant typeface, used for both display and body type. The switch into Times Roman for the word "originals" softens the ad slightly while calling attention to the fact that these pieces are unique, handcrafted items. Futura is not often used for body copy because it is too monotone for easy reading. Here, however, the copy has been heavily leaded, which gives it a very graphic look suited to the ad while improving readability.

Head: Futura Extra Bold 72 pt., tracking: +24, and Times lower case 60 pt., manual letterspacing
Body: Futura Extra Bold 10/20
Logotype: Futura Extra Bold 14/16, tracking: +12, and Futura Extra Bold 11/14, tracking: +12

Trendy, Upscale

This ad capitalizes on contrasts to promote the merchandise and image of a trendy, upscale jewelry store ad. The square ad shape contrasts with the large graphic suggesting round earrings. A great deal of action is added by contrasting values. The choppy black-and-white border works with the interplay of the condensed black and the light weight typefaces to create this effect.

Even though the type is smaller than the rest of the headline and part of the logo, setting "originals" in reversed type gives it the most emphasis. The very condensed serif is reminiscent of a high fashion magazine layout to reinforce the idea that Libby's is the fashionable place to shop.

Head: Bauer Bodoni 120 pt., horizontal scaling: 57%, tracking: +24, and Helvetica Black Condensed 34 pt., manual letterspacing
Body: Bauer Bodoni 11/30, horizontal scaling: 70%
Logotype: Bauer Bodoni 54 pt., horizontal scaling: 50%, tracking: +12, and Helvetica Black Condensed 24 pt., tracking: +35

A TASTE OF ITALY

Three generations of the Scarlotti family in the original bar.

FOR OVER FIFTY YEARS,

THE SCARLOTTI FAMILY HAS OFFERED THE FINEST
FOOD AND WINES FROM ITALY NUMMY NIBH EUIS-
MOD TINCIDUNT UT LAOREET DOLORE MAGNA ALI-
QUAM ERAT VOLUTPAT. UT WISI ENIMAD MINIM
VENIAM, QUIS NOSTRUD EXERCI TATION ULLAMCOR-
PER SUSCIPIT LOBORTIS NISL UT ALIQUIP EX EA COM-
MODO CONSEQUAT. DUIS AUTEM VEL EUM IRIURE
DOLOR IN HENDRERIT IN VULPUTATE UT WISI ENI-
MAD MINIM VENIAM, QUIS NOSTRUD EXERCI TATION
ULLAMCORPER SUSCIPIT LOBORTIS NISL

Scarlotti's

18 West Front Street

☛ For the best in Northern Italian cuisine come to our
new location on ☛ the Square next door to libby's new
york originals where everything's happening.
Try our great ☛ fettucini, salads, veal parmigiana,
seafood ravioli ☛ and our other fine
specialties. a ☛ cup of espresso or cappuccino makes a
great dessert better.

Pasta&More

☛ For the best in Northern Italian cuisine come to our
new location on ☛ the Square next door to libby's new
york originals where everything's happening.
Try our great ☛ fettucini, salds, veal parmigiana,
seafood ravioli ☛ and our other fine
specialties. a ☛ cup of espresso or cappuccino makes a
great dessert better.

Classic Flourish

Here the type gives the ad a classic look. Either Palatino or
Garamond would create that effect and work well set in
caps and small caps, but Palatino has a little more flourish.
Note the flair of the *Y*, for example. The font is left in its
natural proportions and generously tracked to maintain its
classic proportions. You can set small amounts of body
copy in small caps, but try to keep the line lengths short
and use ample leading to ensure readability.

All the type and the graphic are centered within the ad
for a formal, symmetrical look. This also helps pull the eye
down through the ad from the headline to the logo. The
strong subhead should help draw readers into the copy. The
classic look is completed with a traditional, double-ruled
border and a softening rounded frame for the photo. If color
is available, a parchment tinted background and sepia duo-
tone would be the right choices.

Head: Palatino small caps 48 pt., centered
Subheads: Palatino small caps 18/18, centered
Body: Palatino small caps 12/18, centered
Caption: Palatino Italic 9/11
Logotype: Palatino Italic 36 pt., centered, and Palatino
Italic 12/24, centered

Lively, Contemporary

This restaurant needs a distinctive, eye-catching ad that will
be relatively inexpensive to produce so it can run in many
places to build awareness. A lively, contemporary look is
achieved by treating this all-type ad as a play on black and
white, thick and thin. The 6-point dashed border creates a
high contrast frame for the headline which is placed in an
unexpected place—the middle of the copy. *Pasta*, the key
word, is emphasized in Syntax Ultra Black. There's plenty
of white space all around the copy to make it look clean
and stand out in a crowded newspaper.

Bodoni's thicks and thins and low x-height mean that it
is not the most legible of typefaces, but legibility is not a
primary concern for this young audience. The bold graphic
look is carried through with the use of heavy dingbats that
create a choppy rhythm.

Head: Syntax Ultra Black and Syntax, both 36 pt., kerning: -4
Body: Bodoni 12/24

Great Pasta... in 4 minutes for 4 Bucks... ...No Kidding!

New Menu

Molestie consequat, vel illum dolore eu feugiat nulla facilisis at vero eros et accumsan et iusto odio dignissim qui blandit praesent luptatum zzril delenit augue duis dolore te feugait nulla facilisi. Lorem ipsum dolor sit amet, consectetuer adipiscing elit, sed diam nonummy nibh euismod tincidunt ut laoreet dolore magna aliquam erat volutpat. Ut wisi enim ad minim veniam, quis nostrud exerci tation ullamcorper suscipit

lobortis nisl ut aliquip ex ea commodo consequat. Duis autem vel eum iriure dolor in hendrerit in vulputate velit esse consequat,wi dolor sit amet,

Salad Bar

consectetuer adipiscing elit, sed diam nonummy nibh euismod tincidunt ut laoreet dolore magna aliquam erat volutpat. Ut wisi enim ad minim

Scarlotti's
4th & Elm

veniam, quis nostrud exerci tation ullamcorper suscipit lobortis nisl ut aliquip ex ea commodo consequat. Duis autem vel eum iriure dolor in hendrerit in vulputate velit esse molestie consequat,Ut wisi enim ad minim veniam, quis nostrud exerci tation ullamcorper suscipit lobortis nisl ut aliquip exUt

More Toppings

wisi enim ad minim veniam, quis nostrud exerci tation ullamcorper suscipit lobortis nisl ut aliquip com-

---

Your Special Occasion Deserves an Evening of Fine Dining

Tonight sum dolor sit amet, consectetuer adipiscing elit, sed diam nonummy nibh euismod tincidunt ut laoreet dolore magna aliquam erat volutpat. Ut wisi enim ad minim veniam, quis nostrud quis exerci tation ullamcorper suscipit lobortis.

A spectacular view Lorem ipsum dolor sit amet, consectetuer adipiscing elit, sed diam nonummy nibh euismod tincidunt ut laoreet dolore magna aliquam erat volutpat. Lorem ipsum dolor sit amet, consectetuer adipiscing elit, sed diam nonummy nibh euismod tincidunt ut laoreet dolore magna aliquam erat volutpat. Ut wisi enim ad minim veniam, quis nostrud exerci tation ullamcorper suscipit lobortis.

Scarlotti's
Five Riverview Plaza

"Tabloid" Look

Nothing grabs the business crowd's attention like a bold promise set tabloid newspaper style. In this case, Futura Extra Bold Condensed is the "hit 'em over the head" face of choice.

Times is a no-nonsense, readable serif; Palatino would be too delicate. The Times body type is condensed slightly for readability in the narrower column width; this helps prevent some bad line breaks. The strong subheads, set in the headline face, call the reader's attention to the copy as well as break it into more digestible chunks for quick reading. The dark, assertive typeface also draws attention to the name of the restaurant, which might otherwise have been buried under the weight of all that copy. Setting the logo in larger type would have thrown off the balance of the ad's layout.

Head: Futura Extra Bold Condensed 60/56
Subheads: Futura Extra Bold Condensed 18/20
Body: Times Roman 11/16, horizontal scaling: 90%
Logotype: Futura Extra Bold Condensed, 18 pt.
Address: Futura 14/20

Classy, Romantic

To create a classy, romantic mood, this ad uses delicate weights of Bauer Bodoni and Optima in a flush left, rag right setting. The small, single image—presumably of a dramatic skyline or a beautiful, romantic couple seated in the restaurant—will be the focal point with no competition from a bold weight type.

Bauer Bodoni has an exceptionally attractive italic that gives just the right amount of emphasis to the headline and the name of the restaurant here. Surrounding the delicate typeface with a sea of white space subtly emphasizes the message. The large initial caps in Bauer Bodoni carry the typographic theme from the headline through the copy. The caps are a nice complement to the shimmering Optima copy.

Head: Bauer Bodoni Italic 32/38
Initial Caps: Bauer Bodoni Italic 36 pt.
Body: Optima 12/18 flush left, rag right
Logotype: Bauer Bodoni Italic 24 pt. and 14/20

Old-Fashioned, Festive

The festival aspect of a local art show is emphasized here. The slightly condensed Goudy set in small caps has an old-fashioned, festive look meant to create a feeling of nostalgia for the time when the circus coming to town was a major community event. The violator in a solid circle is reminiscent of a balloon.

The old-fashioned look is continued in the body copy, which is also set in Goudy. The subheads have been set in Futura Condensed Extra Bold so they will be visible without having to be set on a separate line. The copy is short enough that the subheads can also take the place of paragraph indents, keeping the copy area subdued so it won't distract from the headline and the graphic effects.

Head: Goudy small caps 116 pt., horizontal scaling: 90%, and 60/60, horizontal scaling: 90%, and Futura Extra Bold 36/50
Violator: Futura Extra Bold 36/50
Subheads in Text: Futura Condensed Extra Bold 16/18
Body: Goudy 12/18
Logotype: Goudy small caps 36/32, horizontal scaling: 90%

Sophisticated & Friendly

Art is emphasized over the festival aspects here. A sophisticated, artistic look is achieved with the generously tracked Futura Extra Bold set in all caps for the "between the lines" information. The Palatino Italic projects an air of elegance because of its calligraphic letterforms without implying that this is a stuffy, highbrow event, as would Weiss. The symmetrical, formal balance is the traditional look for a cultural event, but the short lines of type make the layout more active and actually create some interesting shapes. This ad is still very accessible and friendly even if it doesn't have the fun look of the first.

Head: Futura Extra Bold all caps 18/50, centered, Futura Extra Bold small caps 96/50 (*Art*), Palatino Italic 120/50 (*fest*) with the whole line set centered, and Palatino Italic 54/60, centered
Subheads: Futura Extra Bold small caps 12/20, centered
Body: Palatino 12/18, centered

Tradition, Nostalgia

A homier look is appropriate when crafts are part of the event. So this ad has been designed to convey a sense of tradition and nostalgia. The lead-in is reversed out of two bars with a strong, simple, almost handcarved effect like an address plate. The copy is simple, with no heavy emphasis through weight changes. Featured events are emphasized only by placement on a separate line.

Century Schoolbook is often used to create a home/childhood feeling for readers, but Century is the better choice here. There is enough similarity between the two faces to evoke nostalgia, but Century is a little more sophisticated looking and therefore more appropriate for the arts aspect of the event. Although Helvetica can be a little bland in the regular weight, in the black weight it is strong and dynamic enough to add just the right touch to this ad.

Lead In: Helvetica Black 18/70, tracking: +33, centered
Head: Century Italic small caps and u/lc 106/70
Subhead: Century Italic 48/70, centered
Date: Helvetica Black 18 pt., centered
Body: Century 12/16, centered

Dynamic, Graphic Play

This arts festival of serious, experimental art, music and drama wants to attract more of a mainstream audience. The open lines and the spaces between letters create a dynamic graphic play of black and white. The short bar, which could print in a color or a percentage of black, surprises the eye and reinforces the headline. The asymmetrical balance of the layout is active and energetic; a formal, symmetrical layout like those used in the other Artfest ads is more static.

A contemporary statement is made with generously tracked, strongly condensed Bauer Bodoni, which is very graphic with its thicks and thins. The body copy is set on long enough lines to create an interesting texture, but the lines are still short enough to keep the type readable.

Lead In: Helvetica Black 18/40, tracking: +33
Head: Bauer Bodoni 144/70 and Helvetica Black Condensed 60/70, both with horizontal scaling: 70%
Subhead: Helvetica Black Condensed 36/70, horizontal scaling: 70%, Helvetica Black Condensed caps 36/40, and Helvetica Black Condensed 36/40, manual letterspacing
Date: Helvetica Black Condensed 14/40, tracking: +28
Body: Bauer Bodoni 14/30

Cincinnati Zoo and Botanical Garden's Spring Floral Festival

Agency: Mann Bukvic Associates
Creative Director: David Bukvic
Art Director: Diane Durban
Half-page newspaper ad
Fonts: Copperplate and Sabon
This ornate ad conjures up images of elaborate formal gardens without relying on a more predictable approach—photography. The mood is set with type and the elaborate, floral, decorative border.

Kenwood Towne Center

Agency: Mann Bukvic Associates
Creative Director: David Bukvic
Art Director: Cathy Bertke
Half-page newspaper ad
Fonts: Futura, Lucian, Metropolis, Murray Hill Bond, Helvetica, Bauer Bodoni, Sabon
This ad is designed to appeal to a young woman looking for current European fashion, and borrows from the '60s, also a fashion trend, with strong, contrasting type styling. The look supports the message—fun with an international flair.

You can't hide, but then why would you? With fresh oranges, lemons and limes, the new Spring look is flat-out arresting. Sun-kissed colors. ✱ Dramatic new designs that dance boldly around tradition. *m* They're here, now. Some sweet. Some unabashedly sexy. All are most decidedly brand new. ▣ Skirts that go to great lengths all in the name of style. Skirts that go to short lengths for the very same reason. ⌇ Denim like you've never seen it before; stitched, quilted, up-scale or casual. ⊠ Cool beads. Fun metallics. Soft plaids. Outrageous patterns. It's the season's most talked about trends in the city's most talked about stores. All at Kenwood Towne Centre. Stop by 'cause Spring is definitely in the air. ▱ And it'll be on our runway this Saturday, during our Spring Fashion review. We'll see you there. ◉ Kenwood Towne Centre. Exit 12 off I-71. **Expect The Unexpected.**

FASHION SHOWS Saturday 1&3 pm.

Kenwood Towne Centre

Kenwood Towne Center
Agency: Mann Bukvic Associates
Creative Director: David Bukvic
Art Director: Teresa Newberry
Full-page newspaper ad
Fonts: Placard Bold Condensed, Schneidler Italic
The generously leaded text anchors a variety of visuals that attract and surprise the eye with their placement and scale.

A Taste of Asia

Agency: Mann Bukvic Associates
Creative Director: David Bukvic
Art Director: Carol Bruggemeier
Half-page newspaper ad
Fonts: Nicholas Cochin, Casa Blanca, Sabon
A stylized, elongated sans serif and carefully placed visuals attract the eye. The more antiquated serif body face has an Old World feel.

IF YOU SUSPECT THAT GOOD
LOOKS AND COMFORT ARE INCOMPATIBLE,
WE INVITE YOU TO LOOK AGAIN.

If walking comfortably while looking good is something you've only dreamed of, Rockport has the answer: our new walking pump, combining superbly crafted comfort with the elegant styling of a classic Italian dress shoe. In creating this sleek, fashionable pump, we've adapted the innovative design of our famous walking shoes to give **Rockport**® you the cushioning and support you need to get through a long day on your feet. Experience the Rockport tradition: our look has changed, but our dedication to comfort has not.

Rockports make you
feel like walking

Rockport
Studio: Concrete
Art Director: Diti Katona, John Pylypczak
Design: Diti Katona
Full-page magazine ad
Font: Weiss
The logo typeface is not used for either the body or the headline of this elegant ad as is done in many image ads. Weiss is more crisp but not too formal.

The Royal Viking Line—Unparalleled Luxury
Agency: Goodby Berlin & Silverstein
Creative Directors: Rich Silverstein, Jeffrey Goodby
Art Director: Rich Silverstein
Copywriter: Bob Kerstetter
Photographer: Nadav Kander, Duncan Sim
© Royal Viking Line 1992
Fonts: RVL Gothic, Bernhard Modern Italic
Bernhard Modern has a delicate, classic look, especially when generously leaded and used with a special designed ultra condensed gothic face that has a '20s feeling. (RVL Gothic was designed for Royal Viking Lines and is used in much of their advertising.)

Specialized Bicycles—Welcome Back to the Future

Agency: Goodby Berlin & Silverstein
Creative Directors: Rich Silverstein, Jeffrey Goodby
Art Director: David Page
Copywriter: Dave O'Hare
Photographer: Paul Franz-Moore
© Specialized Bicycles
Fonts: Cochin

A classic typeface contrasts nicely with the condensed sans serif italic logo. The classic, heavily leaded approach with modern, sophisticated text wraps fits the message that this new bike represents a return to classic quality.

The 9th unwritten law of driving

THE ATTRACTION OF
SHOPPING CARTS TO AUTOMOBILES
IS AMONG THE STRONGEST FORCES IN THE UNIVERSE

This being the way of things, we give every new Trooper five coats of tough shopping cart-resistant, space-aged stuff. Then we paint the parts only the road sees four times. Nine coats in all. Then we bake it. Because even with a 190 horse dual overhead cam engine* and rear multi-link/coil suspension, a parked Trooper must be able to survive shopping carts, artistic birds and the car doors of those who long to be close to you.

ISUZU
Practically Amazing

Isuzu Trooper—Shopping Carts

Agency: Goodby Berlin & Silverstein
Creative Directors: Rich Silverstein, Jeffrey Goodby
Art Director: Erich Joiner
Copywriter: Scott Burns
Photographer: Duncan Sim
Illustrator: Alan Daniels
© American Isuzu Motors, Inc.
Fonts: Trajan and Kennerly

Trajan (a face designed only in all caps) creates an elegant, timeless quality that is perfect for the powerful photography. Kennerly is a friendly read for the body copy once the Trajan has gotten your attention.

Brochures

The brochure format is the most flexible of the formats described in this book. A brochure can be virtually any size and can be either folded or bound. A small college or nonprofit agency may use a standard 11" x 8½" sheet folded twice to fit into a #10 envelope or folded, sealed and labeled to be sent as a self-mailer. An industrial brochure can be a lavish, full size, full color project that acts as a showpiece and is often included with other pieces in a sales kit.

Because it is usually unsolicited, the audience should feel the brochure provides value with information and/or should get an impression of quality from attractive visuals and high quality production. Often the format is driven by what the competition is doing and costs. If the brochure is mailed to a large list of prospects, the size and weight of the finished piece will affect both printing and mailing costs. If the brochure is carried by salespeople or is mailed to a few select customers of a big ticket item, there will be fewer production-related budget constraints.

Type Considerations

Since a brochure contains more sales information than an ad, it is important to organize that information for the consumer with heads and subheads or in a question-and-answer format, so the reader doesn't have to wade through all the copy to find the key points. Establish a clear hierarchy of information through your type treatment. Where copy relates to a single product photo, it should be placed near the product, or keyed to the product. Highlight benefits of a product or organization in bulleted or other callout form.

Since the brochure is a sales piece, the type should enhance the sales message or mood. There's more freedom to use a highly stylized type treatment than there is with an editorial format. Consider the market for the product or service and choose type styles that will appeal to the target audience. Choose faces that are in keeping with the image the organization wants to portray—contemporary, chic (for specialty, retail businesses), trend setting, intellectual (for arts organizations), trustworthy, caring (for hospitals).

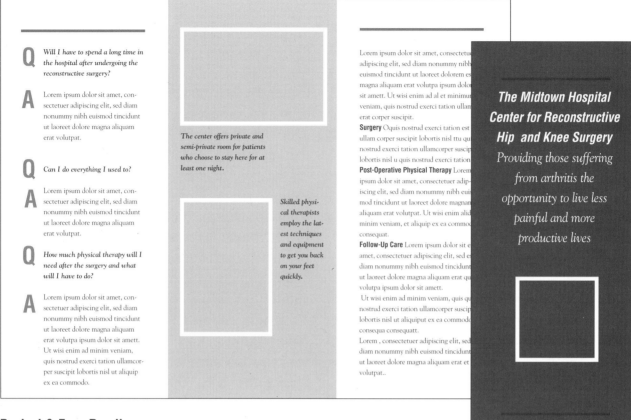

Q *Will I have to spend a long time in the hospital after undergoing the reconstructive surgery?*

A Lorem ipsum dolor sit amet, consectetuer adipiscing elit, sed diam nonummy nibh euismod tincidunt ut laoreet dolore magna aliquam erat volutpat.

Q *Can I do everything I used to?*

A Lorem ipsum dolor sit amet, consectetuer adipiscing elit, sed diam nonummy nibh euismod tincidunt ut laoreet dolore magna aliquam erat volutpat.

Q *How much physical therapy will I need after the surgery and what will I have to do?*

A Lorem ipsum dolor sit amet, consectetuer adipiscing elit, sed diam nonummy nibh euismod tincidunt ut laoreet dolore magna aliquam erat volutpa ipsum dolor sit amett. Ut wisi enim ad minim veniam, quis nostrud exerci tation ullamcorper suscipit lobortis nisl ut aliquip ex ea commodo.

The center offers private and semi-private room for patients who choose to stay here for at least one night.

Skilled physical therapists employ the latest techniques and equipment to get you back on your feet quickly.

Lorem ipsum dolor sit amet, consectetuer adipiscing elit, sed diam nonummy nibh euismod tincidunt ut laoreet dolorem es magna aliquam erat volutpa ipsum dolor sit amet. Ut wisi enim ad al et minimum veniam, quis nostrud exerci tation ullam erat corper suscipit.

Surgery Oquis nostrud exerci tation est ullam corper suscipit lobortis nisl ttu qui nostrud exerci tation ullamcorper suscip lobortis nisl u quis nostrud exerci tation

Post-Operative Physical Therapy Lorem ipsum dolor sit amet, consectetuer adipiscing elit, sed diam nonummy nibh euismod tincidunt ut laoreet dolore magnan aliquam erat volutpat. Ut wisi enim alid minim veniam, et aliquip ex ea commod consequat.

Follow-Up Care Lorem ipsum dolor sit e amet, consectetuer adipiscing elit, sed diam nonummy nibh euismod tincidunt ut laoreet dolore magna aliquam erat qu volutpa ipsum dolor sit amett.
Ut wisi enim ad minim veniam, quis qu nostrud exerci tation ullamcorper suscip lobortis nisl ut aliquiput ex ea commodo consequa consequatt.
Lorem , consectetuer adipiscing elit, sed diam nonummy nibh euismod tincidunt ut laoreet dolore magna aliquam erat et volutpat..

The Midtown Hospital Center for Reconstructive Hip and Knee Surgery
Providing those suffering from arthritis the opportunity to live less painful and more productive lives

Packed & Easy Reading

The main challenge in this brochure was to present a lot of information in an attractive package. This typical three-panel brochure uses a question-and-answer format to address the most commonly asked questions about arthritis and available treatments. The format is often set with the questions in a sans serif (sometimes even the bolder weights) and the answers in a serif. Here, the Goudy Black Italic combined with the Helvetica Black Condensed *Q*'s and *A*'s clearly separates the questions from the answers, set in Goudy, but gives more of a unified look to this panel.

The copy on the far right panel describes the services offered by the center and discusses insurance coverage. A lot of copy must be presented in a legible form. Keep in mind the target audience's age; in this case, an older audience suggests a readable serif for inside copy.

Front Panel

Headline: Helvetica Black Condensed 20/30, centered
Subhead: Goudy Italic 20/30, centered

Inside Panels

Initial Caps: Helvetica Black Condensed 36 pt.
Captions: Goudy Bold Italic 11/16
Questions: Goudy Bold Italic 11/16
Answers: Goudy 11/16
Subheads: Helvetica Bold Condensed 11/16
Body: Goudy 11/16

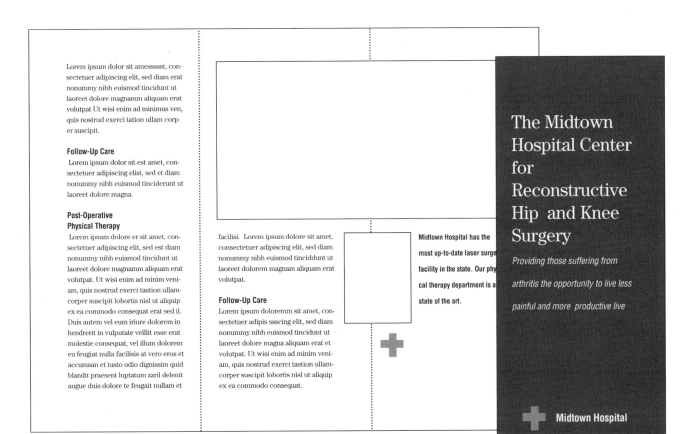

Lorem ipsum dolor sit amessssst, consectetuer adipiscing elit, sed diam erat nonummy nibh euismod tincidunt ut laoreet dolore magnamm aliquam erat volutpat Ut wisi enim ad minimus ven, quis nostrud exerci tation ullam corper suscipit.

Follow-Up Care
Lorem ipsum dolor sit est amet, consectetuer adipiscing elist, sed et diam nonummy nibh euismod tinciderunt ut laoreet dolore magna.

Post-Operative Physical Therapy
Lorem ipsum dolore er sit amet, consectetuer adipiscing elit, sed est diam nonummy nibh euismod tincidunt ut laoreet dolore magnamm aliquam erat volutpat. Ut wisi enim ad minim veniam, quis nostrud exerci tastion ullamcorper suscipit lobortis nisl ut aliquip ex ea commodo consequat erat sed il. Duis autem vel eum iriure dolorem in hendrerit in vulputate velllit esse erat molestie consequat, vel illum dolorem eu feugiat nulla facilisis at vero eros et accumsan et iusto odio dignissim quid blandit praesent luptatum zzril delenit augue duis dolore te feugait nullam et

facilisi. Lorem ipsum dolore sit amet, consectetuer adipiscing elit, sed diam nonummy nibh euismod tinciddunt ut laoreet dolorem magnam aliquam erat volutpat.

Follow-Up Care
Lorem ipsum doloremm sit amet, consectetuer adipis ssscing elit, sed diam nonummy nibh euismod tincidunt ut laoreet dolore magna aliquam erat et volutpat. Ut wisi enim ad minim veniam, quis nostrud exerci tastion ullamcorper suscipit lobortis nisl ut aliquip ex ea commodo consequat.

Midtown Hospital has the most up-to-date laser surge facility in the state. Our phy cal therapy department is a state of the art.

The Midtown Hospital Center for Reconstructive Hip and Knee Surgery

Providing those suffering from arthritis the opportunity to live less painful and more productive live

Midtown Hospital

Clean, Contemporary

This brochure is also for a medical center serving middle-aged and mature adults. But here, a clean, contemporary look is achieved without losing much legibility. This brochure is more suitable for a center that emphasizes the latest technology and wants to project a scientific image.

The key elements of this layout are the white space, a more complicated grid, fewer and larger photos, and a logo used as a graphic in lieu of a small photo on the cover. A more open serif is used for the body and a more heavily leaded sans serif for display copy. Century is a friendly, readable face, but it has sturdier proportions than Goudy and a slightly more modern look. Helvetica Condensed Italic is somewhat less legible than Helvetica Black Condensed because of the slanting letters, but the subheads and caption are short enough that this isn't a real problem.

Front Panel
Headline: Century 27/34
Subhead: Helvetica Condensed Italic 14/34

Inside Panel
Subheads: Helvetica Bold Condensed 12/16
Captions: Helvetica Black Condensed 11/24
Body: Century 11/16
Logotype: Helvetica Bold Condensed 16/34

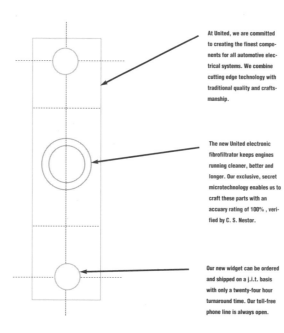

Duis autem vel eum aute iriure dolor in hendrerit in vulp
utate velit esse molestie consequat, vel illum dolore feugiat
nulla facilisis at vero eros esst
accumsan et iusto odio digniss-
sim qui blandit praesent lupp
tatum zzril delenit augue duis
dolore te feugait nulla.

■ Duis quod erat quis quae
   exercotatopm terras erat
   quod erat demos.
■ Ut wisi nulla excita tation
   corper coporum erat sedes
   nonummy nihil bono tuuse
   erat quod quid.
■ Lorem ipsum corpoer et.
   dolorem magnam sed ipso
   nulla nullam.
■ Lorem ipsum nullam corper
   dolore ut nisi nihil bonus et
   auve erat.

   Lorem ipsum dolor sit
amet, consectetuer adipiscing
elit, sed diam nonummy nibh
euismod tincidunt ut laoreet
dolore magna aliquam erat
volutpat. Ut wisi enim ad
minim veniam, quis nostrud
exerci tation ullamcorper suscipit lobortis nisl.

At United, we are committed
to creating the finest components for all automotive elec-
trical systems. We combine
cutting edge technology with
traditional quality and craftsmanship.

The new United electronic
fibrofiltrator keeps engines
running cleaner, better and
longer. Our exclusive, secret
microtechnology enables us to
craft these parts with an
accuary rating of 100% , veri-
fied by C. S. Nestor.

Our new widget can be ordered
and shipped on a j.i.t. basis
with only a twenty-four hour
turnaround time. Our toll-free
phone line is always open.

The Solution

Lorem ipsum doloret sit et
amet, consectetuer adipiscing
elit, sed diam nonummy nibh.
euismod tincidunt ust laoreet
doloret magnam aliquam erat
volutpat. Ut wisi enim ad min
im veniam, quis nostrud exerci tation ullamcorper suscipit
lobortis nisl ut.

■ Lorem ipsum dolor sit amet
   amet consectetuer adipisco
   elit, sed diam nonummy
   nibh.
■ Duis autem vel eum iriure
   dolor in hendrerit in velit
   accusam et iusto odio aliquip
   enim ad veniam.
■ Lorem ipsum dolor. Sit amet
   sed diam nonummy cidunt ut
   eu feugiat.
■ Ut wisi enim ad minim veni
   consectetuer adipising elit
   zzril duis autem.

   Lorem ipsum doloret sit et
amet, consectetuer adipiscing
elit, sed diiam nonummy nibh
euismod tincidunt ustt laoreet
doloret magnam aliquam erat
volutpat. Ut wisi enim ad min
im veniam, quis nostrud exerci tation ullamcorper suscipit
lobortis nisl ut aliquip ex.

Updated Classic Look

This full-size, saddle-stitched brochure achieves some
drama with heavy ink coverage on the cover. The inset
photo should also be dramatic. The bold sans serif *United*
is shown here in white, but the typeface is strong and simple enough to be set in color and reversed out of the dark
background tint.

   Inside, the bold weight of Times is used because it sur-
prints a tint, either a percentage of gray or a color. The type
might even run in a dark tint or fifth color because it is
large and bold enough to still be legible. The combination
of Times and Helvetica is a classic one that business people are familiar and comfortable with. The bold weight of
Times and the Black Condensed version of the Helvetica
make it more updated looking and more interesting.

Cover
Logotype: Helvetica Black Condensed Italic 72 pt.
Subhead: Times Roman Italic 42/54

Interior
Heads: Helvetica Black Condensed 18/20
Captions: Helvetica Black Condensed 11/20
Body: Times Roman Bold 16/20
Bulleted Copy: Times Roman Bold 14/18

United

*advanced technology
for the automotive
industry*

The top portion is a design layout mockup with placeholder Lorem ipsum text.

RECY-CLED PAPERS REALLY SAVE FORESTS & TREES

Lorem ipsum dolor sit amet, consectetuer adipiscing elit, sed diam nonummy nibh euis-mod tincidunt ut laoreet dolor magna aliquam erattt volutpat. Ut wisi enim ad minim veniam, quis nostrud exerci tatation ullamcorper susssscipit lobortis nisl ult aliquip ex ea commodo conse-quat. Duis autem velu eum iriure dolorem in hendrerit in vulputate velit esse molestie con-sequat, vel illum dolore eu feu-giat nulla facilisis at vero eros et accumsan et iusto odio dig-nissim qui blandit praesent luptatum zzril delenit augue duis dolore te feugait nulla facilisi erat ipso est.

Lorem ipsum doloremm sit amet, consectetuer adipiscing elit, sed diam nonummy nibh euismod tincidunt ut laorebeet dolorem magnam aliquam erat volutpat. Lorem ipsum dolore sit amet, consectetuer adipisc-ing elit, sed diamm nonummy

nibh euismod tincidunt ut sede laoreet dolore magnam aliquam erat volutpat. Ut wisit enim add minim veniam, quis qua nostrud exercite tation ullam corper sus-cipit lobortis nislii ut aliquip ex ea commodo consequat.

Duis euis consetquat, velum illum odiom praesent luptatum zzril delenit augue duis dolore te feugait nullam facilisitt. Lorem ipsum dolor sit amet, consecte tetttuer adipiscing elit, sed diam nonummy nibh euismod tin-cidunt ut laoreet dolore.

NorthWest Mills
RECYCLED PAPERS

Renaissance adds a touch of elegance to any project; now available in fifteen colors.

Lorem ipsum dolor situ amet, consectetuer adipiscing elit, sed diam nonummy nibh euis-mod tincidunt ut laoreet dolore magna aliquam erat volutpat. Ut wisi enim ad minim veniam, quis nostrud exerci tation ullamcorper sus-cipit lobortis nisl ut aliquip ex ea commodo consequat. Duis autem vel eum iriure dolor in hendrerit in vulputate velit esse molestie consequat, vel illum dolore eu feugiat nulla facilisis at vero eros et accumsan et iusto odio dignis-sim qui blandit praesent lupta-tum zzril delenit augue duis dolore te feugait nulla facilisi. Lorem ipsum dolor sit amet, consectetuer adipiscing elit, sed diam nonummy nibh euis-mod tincidunt ut laoreet dolore magna aliquam erat volutpat erat est.

Lorem ipsum dolor sit amet, consectetuer adipiscing elit, sed diam nonummy nibh euis-mod tincidunt ut laoreet

dolore magna aliquam erat volutpat. Ut wisi enim ad minim veniam, quis nostrud exerci tation ullamcorper sus-cipit lobortis nisl ut aliquip ex ea commodo consequat. Duis autem vel eum iriure dolor in hendrerit in vulputate velit esse qui blandit praesent lupta-tum zzril delenit augue duis dolore te feugait nulla facilisi. Lorem ipsum dolor sit amet, consectetuer adipiscing magna aliquam erat volutpat.

The flocked surface of Evanescence will add a lovely texture to your next brochure

Homey, Warm Image

This is a very different look for an image piece than the one on the facing page, with a homier, warmer approach to graphics and type. The pattern on the cover resembles a quilt or wrapping paper pattern. The company name is much larger than the rest of the brochure's title. But to compensate, the name of the line is set in Futura Extra Bold small caps, which has a strong presence on any page.

The reversed type is carried through on the interior, but this time against a lighter tint. The boxed type could be either a sidebar or a quote; it's essentially a graphic device to help break up the long opening block of copy. Goudy is used for the body copy. Its old-fashioned look is perfect for the homey, warm image. Futura Extra Bold's strong, very graphic look signals that North West Mills have an eye for what's modern and useful. The tree logo acts as an endstop in a long narrative.

Cover

Title: Goudy 100/96 and 48/96, horizontal scaling: 70%, and Futura Extra Bold small caps 16/24, horizontal scaling: 70%

Interior

Captions: Futura Extra Bold 10/20, horizontal scaling: 70%
Body: Goudy 14/20, centered
Bulleted Copy: Futura Extra Bold 12/20, tracking: +22
Quote/Sidebar: Futura Extra Bold caps 12/24

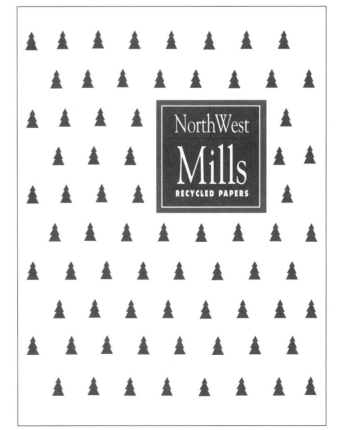

Tuis autem vel eum iri-ure dolor in hendrerit in vulputate velit esse molestie consequat, vel illum dolore eu feugiat nulla facilisis at vero eros et accumsan et iusto odio dignissim qui blandit praesent luptatum zzril delenit augue duis dolore.

Lorem ipsum dolor sit amet, consectetuer adipiscing elit, sed diam nonummy nibh euismod tincidunt ut laoreet dolore magna aliquam erat volutpat. Ut wisi enim ad minim veniam, quis nostrud exerci tation ullamcorper suscipit lobortis nisl ut aliquip ex ea commodo consequat est neq. Lorem ipsum dolor sit amet, consectetuer adipiscing elit, sed diam nonum-my nibh euismod.

Lorem ipsum dolor sit amet, consectetuer adipiscing elit, sed diam nonummy nibh euismod tincidunt ut laoreet dolore magna aliquam erat volutpat. Ut wisi enim ad minim veniam, quis nostrud exerci tation ullamcorper suscipi.

Sarah Bailey
President

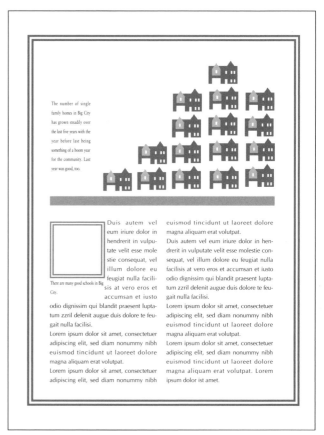

The number of single family homes in Big City has grown steadily over the last five years with the year before last being something of a boom year for the community. Last year was good, too.

There are many good schools in Big City.

Duis autem vel eum iriure dolor in hendrerit in vulpu-tate velit esse mole stie consequat, vel illum dolore eu feugiat nulla facili-sis at vero eros et accumsan et iusto odio dignissim qui blandit praesent lupta-tum zzril delenit augue duis dolore te feu-gait nulla facilisi.

Lorem ipsum dolor sit amet, consectetuer adipiscing elit, sed diam nonummy nibh euismod tincidunt ut laoreet dolore magna aliquam erat volutpat.

Lorem ipsum dolor sit amet, consectetuer adipiscing elit, sed diam nonummy nibh

euismod tincidunt ut laoreet dolore magna aliquam erat volutpat.

Duis autem vel eum iriure dolor in hen-drerit in vulputate velit esse molestie con-sequat, vel illum dolore eu feugiat nulla facilisis at vero eros et accumsan et iusto odio dignissim qui blandit praesent lupta-tum zzril delenit augue duis dolore te feu-gait nulla facilisi.

Lorem ipsum dolor sit amet, consectetuer adipiscing elit, sed diam nonummy nibh euismod tincidunt ut laoreet dolore magna aliquam erat volutpat.

Lorem ipsum dolor sit amet, consectetuer adipiscing elit, sed diam nonummy nibh euismod tincidunt ut laoreet dolore magna aliquam erat volutpat. Lorem ipsum dolor ist amet.

Upscale, Traditional

Typically real estate brochures are actually folders that may contain a number of loose sheets that can be added, changed or given away. It's important, therefore, to estab-lish a strong, memorable identity so the sheets can be easi-ly changed and their source quickly recognized. Here, the Sabon typeface is used for logotype, title and captions to create a definite, unified typographic look. The double ruled border is used on both folder and loose sheets for a simple, yet distinctive identity.

This firm specializes in single occupant dwellings, and wants to convey an upscale, but traditional image. Sabon's letterforms and serifs place it squarely in the ranks of tradi-tional type, and it is quite an elegant face. Optima has a classic, timeless look and a simple, serifless design that gives it a business-like quality.

Cover
Logotype: Sabon 121 pt., horizontal scaling: 70%, tracking: -9, and Sabon 54/78, horizontal scaling: 70%
Title: Sabon 60/78, horizontal scaling: 70%

Interior
Body: Optima 12/18, justified
Captions: Sabon 10/18, horizontal scaling: 70%, justified

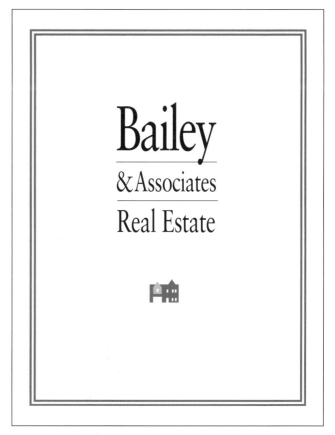

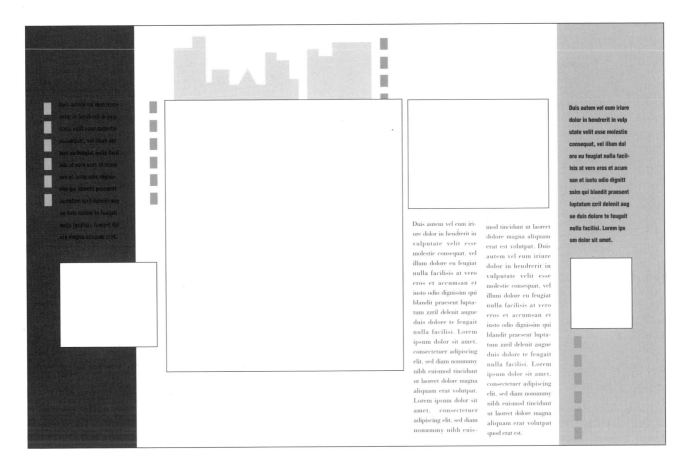

Elegant, Graphic

A graphic, stylized rendition of a city skyline sets the tone for this slick approach to selling real estate. The narrow justified columns echo the shape of the buildings, and the series of windows from the cover graphic are a decorative element that carries through the brochure in open spaces.

The type needs to have a strong graphic look. Bauer Bodoni is both an elegant and a graphic-looking face, which makes it a good choice for a logotype on the cover and the body copy inside. Helvetica Black Condensed is used for the captions because it will hold up better at this point size when reversed. Its geometric design fits well with the blocky graphics.

Cover

Logotype: Bauer Bodoni 120 pt., horizontal scaling: 70%, and Helvetica Black Condensed 24/70, tracking: +53
Title: Helvetica Black Condensed 24/70, tracking: +53

Interior

Body: Bauer Bodoni 12/18, justified
Captions: Helvetica Black Condensed 11/22

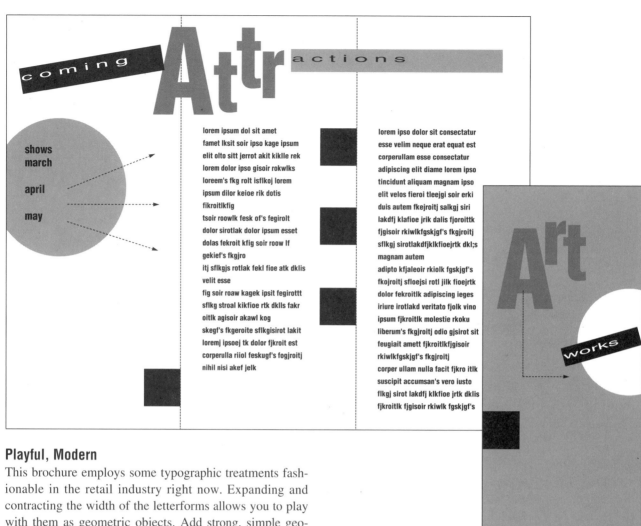

Playful, Modern

This brochure employs some typographic treatments fashionable in the retail industry right now. Expanding and contracting the width of the letterforms allows you to play with them as geometric objects. Add strong, simple geometric shapes in bright colors or several shades of black and gray, and the result is a playful, modern brochure for an arts organization. Place the bold elements carefully, and consider the letters as shapes first; the message is of secondary importance.

Helvetica is so readable (for a sans serif) that you can take a lot of liberties with it. It's sturdy enough that it can be reversed or printed over a tint without losing much readability. Since Helvetica has a large x-height and a strong vertical thrust, even in the condensed version, close, even word spacing is important for the body type.

Front Panel
Title: Helvetica 14 pt., horizontal scaling: 250%, and Helvetica Black Condensed 168 pt. (*A*) and 120 pt. (*rt*), manual letterspacing

Inside Panels
Headline: Helvetica 14 pt., horizontal scaling: 250%, and Helvetica Black Condensed 168 pt. (*A*) and 120 pt. (*ttr*), manual letterspacing
Body: Helvetica Black Condensed 11/18
Subheads: Helvetica Black Condensed 16 pt.

Tobellilorem ipsum dolor sit amet, consectetuer adipiscing elit, sed diam nonummy nibh euismod tincidunt ut laoreet dolore magna alquo iquam erat volutpat. Ut wisi enim ad alia minim veniam, quis nostrud exerci atque tation ullamcorper suscipit lobortis nisl ut aliquip ex ea eam commodo consetr quat. Duis autem vel eum iriure dolor in hendrerit in vulputate velit esse fism

molestie consequat, vel illum dolore eu feugiat nulla facilisis at vero eros et accumsan et iusto odio dignissim qui blandit praesent luptatum zzril delenit feugait nulla facilisi.
Gregorinlorem ipsum dolor sit amet, consectetuer adipiscing elit, sed diam et nonummy nibh euismod tincidunt utt ut laoreet dolore magna aliquam erat voluptpat. Ut wisi enim ad minim veniam, quis nostrud exerci tation ullamcorper suscipit lobortis nisl ut aliqui aliquip ex ea commodo consequat. Ut wisi enim ad minim

veniam, quis nostrud tis nisl ut aliquip ex ea commodo sequat consequat.
Marshalllorem ipsum dolor sit amet, consectetuer adipiscing elit, sed diam et nonummy nibh euismod tincidunt ut alia laoreet dolore magna aliquam erat volutpat. Ut wisi enim ad minim veniam.
Larrabyorem est ipsum dolor sit amet, consectetuer adipiscing elit, sed diam est nonummy nibh euismod tincidunt ut alia laoreet dolore magna aliquam erat volutpat. Ut ullamcorper suscipit consequat.

Naive, Primitive

This gallery brochure has a laid-back, primitive approach. It works well for an informal gallery that focuses on affordable, popular pieces and consciously seeks to interest more people in the arts. The graphics give it a Southwest look, but the type selections would work with another theme. The flush left, rag right copy can rag at the bottom and have a column or two open and still hang together, especially with graphics.

Syntax Ultra Black has great strength and authority—even when condensed and "cut up" as shown here. Syntax and Century both have a naive quality, so they work well together here. While a lighter weight of either the Helvetica or Syntax could have been used for the body copy, a serif is still more readable for this much copy.

Front Panel
Headline: Syntax Ultra Black 120 pt., horizontal scaling: 70%, tracking: +30, and Century 96 pt., horizontal scaling: 50%, tracking: -17
Subhead: Helvetica Black Condensed 18/20, tracking: +12

Inside Panels
Headline: Syntax Ultra Black 120 pt., horizontal scaling: 70%, tracking: +30, and Century 72 pt., horizontal scaling: 50%, tracking: -17
Body: Century 14/20
Subheads: Helvetica Black Condensed 18/20

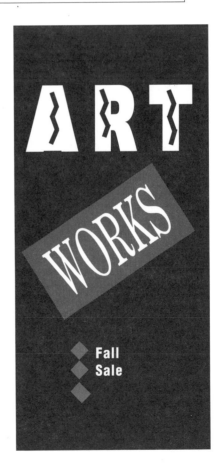

UPTOWN RACQUET CLUB

Lorem ipsum dolor sit amet, consectetuer adipiscing elit, sed diam nonummy nibh euismod tincidunt ut laoreet dolore magna aliquam erat volutpat. Ut wisi enim ad minim veniam, quis nostrud exerci tation ullamcorper suscipit lobortis nisl ut aliquip ex ea commodo consequat. Duis autem vel eum iriure dolor in hendrerit in vulputate velit esse molestie consequat, vel illum dolore eu feugiat nulla facilisis at vero eros et accumsan et iusto odio dignissim qui blandit praesent luptatum zzril delenit augue duis dolore te feugait nulla facilisi. Lorem ipsum dolor sit amet, consectetuer adipiscing elit, sed diam nonummy nibh euismod tincidunt ut laoreet dolore magna ali-

quam erat volutpat erat neq. Ut wisi enim ad minim veniam, quis nostrud exerci tation ullamcorper suscipit lobortis nisl ut aliquip ex ea commodo consequat. Duis autem vel eum iriure dolor in hendrerit

Our inviting facility offers indoor squash and tennis as well as racquetball courts and a beautiful spa.

in vulputate velit esse molestie consequat, vel illum dolore eu feugiat nulla facilisis at vero eros et accumsan et iusto odio dignissim qui blandit praesent luptatum zzril delenit augue duis dolore te feugait nulla facilisi. Nam liber tempor cum soluta nobis eleifend option congue nihil imperdiet doming id quod mazim placerat facer possim assum. Lorem ipsum dolor sit amet, consectetuer adipiscing elit, sed diam nonummy nibh euismod tincidunt ut laoreet dolore magna aliquam erat volutpat. Ut wisi enim ad minim veniam, quis nostrud exerci tation ullamcorper suscipit lobortis nisl ut aliquip ex ea

free trial membership order form

To receive your free trial membership, simply fill out this slip and return it to the address below:

Name

Address

City   *Sate*   *Zip*

Mail to: Uptown Racquet Club

12 Estate Place

Uod mazim 12345

Exclusive, Sophisticated

This membership offer brochure for a health club seeks to project the image of an exclusive, private club. Although the type is restrained, with regatta colors (bright pastels) this brochure could have a strong impact.

The generously tracked Optima for the logotype is reminiscent of engraving on a plaque. The letterforms of the Sabon Italic are elegant. The light, open-looking regular weight is inviting, but this typeface is still more formal looking than Times or Century would be. The combination of the regular and the italic Sabon on the coupon creates the impression that it's an engraved invitation.

Front Panel
Title: Optima Bold caps 34/86, tracking: +80, and Sabon Italic 24/66, horizontal scaling: 70%, centered
Violator: Sabon Italic 24/46, horizontal scaling: 70%

Inside Panels
Headline: Optima Bold caps 24/50, tracking: +70, and Sabon Italic 18/50, horizontal scaling: 70%
Body: Sabon 11/16, justified
Caption: Optima 11/16, centered

Coupon
Headline: Sabon Italic 24/46, centered
Copy: Sabon and Sabon Italic, both 12/26
Form Labels: Sabon Italic 12/16, horizontal scaling: 70%

An exclusive

offer from the

U P T O W N

R A C Q U E T

C L U B

free trial membership

Get in Shape

Lorem ipsum dolor sit amet, consectetuer adipiscing elit, sed diam nonummy nibh euismod tincidunt ut laoreet dolore magna aliquam erat volutpat. Ut wisi enim ad minim veniam, quis nostrud exerci tation ullamcorper suscipit lobortis nisl ut aliquip ex ea commodo consequat. Duis autem vel eum iriure dolor in hendrerit in vulputate velit esse molestie consequat, vel illum dolore eu feugiat nulla facilisis at vero eros et accumsan et iusto odio dignissim qui blandit praesent luptatum zzril delenit augue duis dolore te feugait nulla facilisi. Lorem ipsum dolor sit amet, consectetuer adipiscing elit, sed diam nonummy nibh euismod tincidunt ut laoreet dolore magna aliquam erat volutpat. Ut wisi enim ad minim veniam, quis nostrud exerci tation ullam-

corper suscipit lobortis nisl ut aliquip ex ea commodo consequat. Duis autem vel eum iriure dolor in hendrerit in vulputate velit esse molestie consequat, vel illum dolore eu feugiat nulla facilisis at vero eros et accumsan et iusto odio dignissim qui blandit praesent luptatum zzril delenit augue duis dolore te feugait nulla facilisi.

Meet Friends

Nam liber tempor cum soluta nobis eleifend option congue nihil imperdiet doming id quod mazim placerat facer possim assum. Lorem ipsum dolor sit amet, consectetuer adipiscing elit, sed diam nonummy nibh euismod tincidunt ut laoreet dolore magna aliquam erat volutpat. Ut wisi enim ad minim ve... tation ulla...

Our friendly instructors will help you have a good time while you are getting in shape. Muffy, our head aerobics instructor, will help you frim and tone your body. Biff will help you design the right wieght lifting program for that perfect body.

Upbeat, Active

Health clubs seldom have photographs that are of good enough quality to run large. This design has a lively layout with decorative use of small photos instead. The italic used for heads and body reinforces the upbeat, active nature of the club. The letterforms of Helvetica Condensed Italic have only a slight slant; that's enough to create the desired active look, but not enough to make the body copy hard to read. The flush left, rag right copy creates a feeling of motion from left to right, especially since the large right-hand margin has been maintained even where there are no photos.

Front Panel

Title: Times Roman Italic 70/60, horizontal scaling: 95%
Blurb: Helvetica Bold Condensed Italic 14/40, tracking: +18

Inside Panels

Headline: Times Italic 60/60, horizontal scaling: 95%
Body: Helvetica Condensed Italic 10/16
Caption: Helvetica Condensed Italic 10/24

Lorem ipsum dolor sit amet, consectetuer adipiscing elit, sed diam nonummy nibh euismod tincidunt ut laoreet dolore magna aliquam erat volutpat. Ut wisi enim ad minim veniam, quis nostrud exerci tation ullamcorper suscipit lobortis nisl ut aliquip ex ea commodo consequat.

Duis autem vel eum iriure dolor in hendrerit in vulputate velit esse molestie consequat, vel illum dolore eu feugiat nulla facilisis at vero eros et accumsan et iusto odio dignissim qui blandit praesent luptatum zzril delenit augue duis dolore te feugait nulla facilisi.

Central Quad

dolor sit amet, consectetuer adipiscing elit, sed diam nonummy nibh euismod tincidunt ut laoreet dolore magna aliquam erat volutpat.

Ut wisi enim ad minim veniam, quis nostrud exerci tation ullamcorper suscipit lobortis nisl ut aliquip emequat.

Duis autem vel eum iriure dolor in hendrerit in vulputate velit esse molestie consequat, vel illum dolore eu feugiat nulla facilisis at vero eros et accumsan et iusto odio dignissim

At Atheneum we look toward tomorrow. But we don't forget the past.

qui blandit praesent luptatum zzril delenit augue duis dolore te feugait nulla facilisi.

Computer Center

Nam liber tempor cum soluta nobis eleifend option congue nihil imperdiet

doming id quod mazim placerat facer possim assum. Lorem ipsum dolor sit amet, consectetuer adipiscing elit, sed diam nonummy nibh euismod tincidunt ut laoreet dolore magna aliquam erat volutpat. Ut wisi enim ad minim veniam, quis nostrud exerci tation ullamcorper suscipit lobortis nisl ut aliquip ex ea commodsis.

Tradition & Progress

m dolor sit amet, consectetuer adipiscing elit, sed diam nonummy nibh euismod tincidunt ut laoreet dolore magna aliquam erat volutpat. Ut wisi enim ad minim veniam, quis nostrud exerci tation ullamcorper suscipit lobortis nisl ut aliquip ex ea commodo consequat.

Duis autem vel eum iriure dolor in hendrerit in vulputate velit esse molestie consequat, vel illum dolore eu feugiat nulla facilisis at vero eros et accumsan et iusto odio dignissim qui blandit praesent luptatum zzril

Dynamic Tradition

This design for a small college reflects the image the college wants to project— one of mixing valued traditions with modern technology and sophisticated professors. A simple three-column format inside has a wide margin and a double rule to avoid making this text-heavy piece look too crowded and forbidding. The flush left, rag right setting and the generous leading also help update the brochure graphically. If the leading were tighter and the type set justified or centered, the piece would have a more static, formal—and therefore rather stuffy—look.

Goudy creates the right look for this brochure. It has a nostalgic quality without looking dated. The Helvetica Bold Condensed Italic adds a dynamic, provocative accent.

Front Panel

Headline: Goudy 60/72, horizontal scaling: 80%, and Goudy Italic 48/60, horizontal scaling: 80%

Inside Panels

Initial Cap: Goudy 60 pt.
Body: Goudy 12/18
Subheads: Helvetica Condensed Bold Italic 18/18
Captions: Helvetica Condensed Bold Italic 12/18

Atheneum
College
*Preparing for
the Future*

I could have gone to this major university, but I felt that ATU had the best program in biology.

Lorem ipsum dolor sit amet, consectetuer adipiscing elit, sed diam nonummy nibh euismod tincidunt ut laoreet dolore magna aliquam erat volutpat. Ut wisi enim ad minim veniam, quis nostrud exerci tation ullamcorper suscipit lobortis nisl ut aliquip ex ea commodo consequat.

ATU professors could get high-paying jobs anywhere, but they still make it easy to learn complex subjects.

Duis autem vel eum iriure dolor in hendrerit in vulputate velit esse molestie consequat, vel illum dolore eu feugiat nulla facilisis at vero eros et accumsan et iusto odio dignissim qui blandit praesent luptatum zzril delenit augue duis dolore te feugait nulla facilisi. Lorem ipsum dolor sit amet, consectetuer adipiscing elit, sed diam nonummy nibh euismod tincidunt ut laoreet dolore magna aliquam erat volutpat. Ut wisi enim ad minim veniam,

quis nostrud exerci tation ullamcorper suscipit lobortis nisl ut aliquip ex ea commodo consequat.

Duis autem vel eum iriure dolor in hendrerit in vulputate velit esse molestie consequat, vel illum dolore eu feugiat nulla facilisis at vero eros et accumsan et iusto odio dignissim qui blandit praesent luptatum zzril delenit augue duis dolore te feugait nulla facilisi. Nam liber tempor cum soluta nobis eleifend option congue nihil imperdiet doming id quod mazim

I couldn't believe I'd really have a computer in my dorm room—but I do!

placerat facer possim assum. Lorem ipsum dolor sit amet, consectetuer adipiscing elit, sed diam nonummy nibh euismod tincidunt ut laoreet dolore magna aliquam erat volutpat. Ut wisi enim ad minim veniam, quis nostrud exerci tation ullamcorper suscipit lobortis nisl ut aliquip ex ea commodsis.

Graphic, Contemporary

This brochure is targeted toward students who are considering majors in engineering, science or math. A more contemporary approach has a complicated format with indented pull quotes, and a flush left, rag right orientation throughout. The bleed cover photo and heavier ink coverage complement the more graphic approach.

The university's logo uses Times. Set here in all caps, it looks as if it would be at home on an athlete's letter sweater—a strong, vigorous image. On the inside panels, the Times retains readability even when it is run very small and generously to fit the graphic look. It has fairly compact letterforms that help prevent bad breaks at the ends of lines and where it runs around the quotes. A strong, black sans serif adds contrast and graphic interest in pull quotes and captions.

Front Panel

Headline: Times 96 pt., horizontal scaling: 80%
Subhead: Helvetica Black Condensed Italic 24/48

Inside Panels

Body: Times 12/18
Pull Quotes: Futura Extra Bold Condensed 14/25
Captions: Futura Extra Bold Condensed 14/25

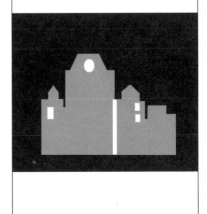

ATU

succeeding,

not just surviving

in the 90's

declare bankruptcy to avoid compensating for the injuries or deaths they have caused. MADD also pressed for the introduction in Congress of two key bills: the Pell amendment, which would give authorities the option to deport aliens convicted of felony DWI; and the Sensible Advertising and Family Education Act, which would extend warnings currently on alcoholic beverage containers to alcohol advertising as well. In May 1991, volunteers who help MADD work for the enactment of such bills received a new Impaired Driving Issues "How To" manual, which will make them even stronger advocates in their communities. More than 230 activists, highway-safety officials, prosecutors, law enforcement officers and others also received training and resource materials on effective drunk-driving countermeasures through MADD workshops around the country.

FOR VICTIMS OF DRUNK DRIVING, a gift to MADD is a gift of hope. That hope comes in many forms and is offered by many people, from professional caregivers to our own carefully trained volunteers. In fiscal year 1990-91, more than 250 MADD victim advocates completed a 40-hour training program at Victim Assistance Institutes, where they

Mothers Against Drunk Driving Annual Report

Designer: Bryan L. Peterson
© 1992 Peterson & Company
Fonts: Copperplate 33 BC, Berkeley Medium
This annual report uses the color olive, notebook pages, and an overall ledger motif. The statistics, in chart form, are the only place red is used. These charts are emphasized with strong graphics and copperplate text reversed out of black bars.

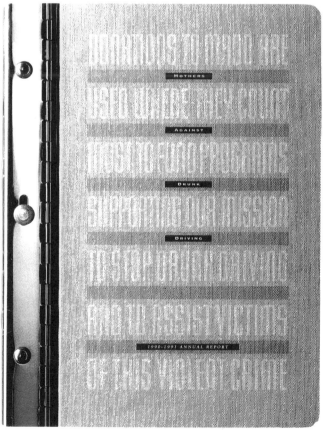

as a percentage of traffic) has improved 30 percent and construction cycle time (the time required to deliver a home) has declined 12 percent, resulting in a faster turn of our assets.

If we execute exactly, we achieve two goals: we complete a zero-defect home and we exceed our customers' expectations. If we do everything right the first time, every time, we will reach our goal of 100 percent "recommendation without reservation."

Centex is dedicated to constant improvement. Our challenge now and in the future is to continue to refine our execution, maintain our quality and achieve complete customer satisfaction as market conditions improve and our home building business expands. Our 3-D approach will make it happen.

A CLASS ACT

During fiscal 1992, Centex Homes committed $2 million to implement its Sales and Marketing, and Production Management training programs. Centex Homes' three on-staff facilitators in that effort are, from left, Jay Kapal, Vice President; Doug Stempowski, Vice President of Sales and Marketing; and

John Ule, Director of Production Development. Traveling to virtually all of our 39 home building divisions for the in-the-field classes, together the trio flew nearly 279,000 miles this past year. Now that's commitment.

MORTGAGE OPERATION BRANCHED OUT AS RATES RETREATED

The lowest interest rates in nearly two decades revived the mortgage markets in fiscal 1992 just as CTX Mortgage Company, our mortgage banking subsidiary, completed a major expansion program. The result was a year of spectacular growth for CTX – an almost 25 percent increase in branch locations to 56 in 1992, all-time-high loan volume, and its most profitable year.

CTX originated and closed a record 23,716 loans – a 40 percent increase over fiscal 1991 loans. Our "builder" (Centex-built) volume of 5,897 units in 1992 was slightly lower than 6,002 units in the prior year, but in both years represented approximately 75 percent of Centex's total home closings. Partly because of a record number of refinancings, our "spot" (third party) business increased 62 percent to 17,819 loans this year versus 10,996 spot loans in the prior year.

Loan origination value totaled $2.5 billion, a 61 percent increase over total origination value in 1991. Operating earnings from our financial services businesses, including our title and hazard insurance operations, reached an all-time high of $19.5 million, more than double the $7.9 million reported in fiscal 1991. This year's earnings improvement was due primarily to the increased volume and higher average loan amounts, combined with record interest rate spreads and favorable hedging opportunities. CTX's earnings were generated from normal ongoing operations and did not include any extraordinary sales or other items.

Although favorable conditions certainly prevailed in the financial markets during the fiscal year, it was CTX's positioning and increased operating efficiency which resulted in its excellent financial performance.

Centex entered the mortgage business in fiscal 1974 to better manage its housing business in the Dallas/Fort Worth area where the majority of the building activity was taking place. Having our own mortgage financing company offered several benefits – knowledge of the status of a customer's loan and coordination of loan approval with the home building process, as well as the added simplification of dealing with just one mortgage company.

When the opportunity occurred in the late 1980's, our loan offices began processing "spot" loans on an incremental basis and CTX subsequently began developing spot-only branches. Currently, spot loans account for about 75 percent of CTX's loan volume.

Being the mortgage financing arm of the nation's largest builder has its advantages. The increasing geographic diversity of Centex's home building operation has provided a natural infrastructure for CTX's growth, and we have a mortgage operation in virtually all of our home building markets. Our home building divisions and their respective builder loan branches work closely with each other to ensure that the building and mortgage financing processes mesh as they should. This results in the best total home buying experience for our customers.

Our mortgage financing strategy has evolved over time. CTX originates mortgage loans, securitizes and sells them, along with the servicing rights, without retaining any loans. Prior to closing, we hedge those mortgages in which rates have been locked. We focus on servicing the customer rather than on price.

CTX earns revenue three ways: on the loan's origination fee; on the positive "carry" between long-term and short-term rates during the required securitization period between loan closing and its delivery to the purchaser; and on the sale of the loan's servicing rights.

As in all of our businesses, the success of our Mortgage Banking operation depends on the quality of our workforce. In addition to our base of long-tenured employees, as a result of the recent mortgage industry consolidation, CTX's expansion and success has attracted a number of very experienced people.

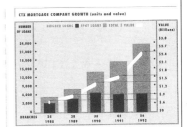

CTX MORTGAGE COMPANY GROWTH (units and value)

In fiscal 1988, CTX Mortgage originated a total of 3,584 loans valued at $462 million. By 1992, originations had more than quadrupled to 23,716 with a total value of $2.5 billion.

150

and still going and going....

Who says there's no such thing as a "perfect house?" Not Jim Drowdy, a Field Manager in Centex Homes' Tampa division, and certainly not his customers.

Perfection is a habit with Jim. Over the past three years, Jim and his crew have delivered 150 zero-defect homes to customers at the time of pre-settlement. On an average of about once a week they deliver to a customer a completed Centex home which the customer considers perfect,

with no items in need of repair.

What is Jim's "secret?" "There are no secrets," he says, "just dedication, commitment, spending time getting to know your customers so you can meet their needs and expectations, and teamwork – all the things we learned in production management training. I won't sacrifice quality for speed and I don't take shortcuts. I won't accept any excuse for inferior work. There isn't any."

Apparently not.

Centex Corporation Annual Report 1992

Designer: Bryan L. Peterson
© 1992 Peterson & Company
Fonts: Berkeley Medium, Franklin Gothic Bold, Futura Bold Condensed

Illustrations, outlined halftones of officers, charts and sidebars break up the text in this annual report. The effect is dynamic and encourages readership with type treatment that is reminiscent of a consumer magazine.

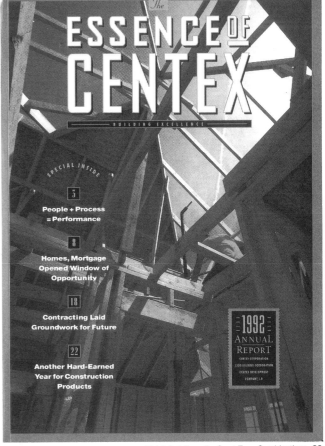

News Release

For Immediate Release
Contact: *(Name and phone number)*

'Healthy People' Coming to Town

NAME OF TOWN OR CITY *(date)* — Community residents will have a chance to join in a national effort to improve America's health when *(name of hospital)* brings Healthy People 2000 to *(name of community)*.

Healthy People 2000, sponsored by the U.S. Public Health Service (USPHS), is a nationwide strategy aimed at improving America's health status by the turn of the century. The initiative is based on health promotion and disease prevention objectives released by USPHS in September 1990. National goals are set for reducing death, disease, and disability by the year 2000 in 21 priority areas, including maternal and child health; cancer, stroke, and heart disease prevention; prevention of unintentional injuries; and drug and alcohol abuse prevention.

(Name of hospital) will work with community leaders to identify local health risks that should be addressed so (name of community) can contribute to a healthier America by the year 2000.

"Our goal is to provide information, resources, and programs to enable the members of our community to make better choices about their health and lifestyles," said *(name of hospital spokesman)*. An estimated two-thirds of Americans die prematurely of preventable illness and injury.

(Name of hospital) joins hospitals across the country in participating in Healthy People 2000.

# # #

thirty-six

Fact Sheet

Here are some facts and figures that underscore the need for the Healthy People 2000 program. An excellent resource for national statistics is *Health United States 1989*, published by the U.S. Department of Health and Human Services. It is available for $19.00 from the Superintendent of Documents, U.S. Government Printing Office, Washington, DC 20402 (stock number 017-022-01104-2). Visa or Mastercard orders will be accepted at 202/783-3238. Whenever possible, supplement national information with local data.

The Choices We Make...

Two out of three deaths and one in three hospital stays are linked to six personal health risks: tobacco, alcohol, injury, high blood pressure, overnutrition (as measured by obesity and high blood cholesterol), and gaps in primary medical care.
THE CARTER CENTER OF EMORY UNIVERSITY, 1984

In 1987, 29 percent of adults 18 and over smoked cigarettes. The less educated are at higher risk. Between 1974 and 1987, smoking among persons 25 and over declined by only 7 percent for those with less than a high school education; 39 percent of college graduates quit.
NATIONAL CENTER FOR HEALTH STATISTICS, 1989

In 1987, an estimated 105,000 persons died from alcohol-related causes — 4.9 percent of all U.S. deaths.
CENTERS FOR DISEASE CONTROL, 1990

Although wearing a seat belt can significantly reduce risk of injury in an automobile accident, less than half of us wear them regularly.
NATIONAL SAFETY COUNCIL, 1989

Motorcycle riders who don't wear helmets are two to three times more likely to suffer head and neck injuries than those who do.
NATIONAL HIGHWAY TRAFFIC SAFETY ADMINISTRATION, 1988

...And the Price of Those Choices

A 40-year-old man who smokes two packs of cigarettes a day, does not exercise or wear a seat belt, and is 30 percent overweight had medical bills of $1,282 in 1988, twice that of a man with healthier habits.
CONTROL DATA CORP, 1989

Treatment for smoking-related diseases cost Americans more than $23 billion in 1984.
AMERICAN LUNG ASSOCIATION, 1987

Alcohol abuse will generate $136.3 billion in health care costs in 1990 — half again the amount of federal spending on Medicare patients in 1988. Average monthly health care costs for alcoholics are twice as high as for nonalcoholics.
AMERICAN MEDICAL ASSOCIATION, 1988

thirty-seven

At the heart of Healthy People 2000 is recognition that individual decisions, supported by community action, add up to health for our nation.

American Hospital Association Healthy People 2000

Art Director/Designer: Mark Oldach

Fonts: Futura, Garamond

The high contrast approach with grainy halftones is complemented in this black on white booklet with black spiral binding and Futura heads and initial caps. Sidebars reverse out of black in Garamond Italic. Half-sheets present information, while bold graphics entice the reader further into the booklet.

Healthy People 2000

America's Hospitals Respond

A resource kit to help you mobilize a community-wide health promotion initiative linked to national Year 2000 objectives.

American Hospital Association

Community Programs

Participation in community programs and events:

• Donate hospital managers' time to serve on the boards of community organizations. Offer strategic planning assistance to community groups; it will help you stay in touch with their issues.

• Encourage employees to volunteer for community organizations by recognizing those who do so with a distinctive pin or button or at the annual banquet. Use meetings with other managers, publications, and special announcements to generate awareness and pride in employees' contributions to the community.

• Open a hospital meeting room to community meetings, educational classes, forums, and other gatherings. Use these as opportunities to distribute materials presenting the hospital as a vital community resource.

• Be sure your hospital is represented at community events such as holiday parades, street fairs, and so on. Provide blood pressure screenings, literature on health topics, handouts about the hospital. Be where you are not expected, too. Set up a hot chocolate or lemonade stand (depending on the season) offering refreshments to commuters. Or hand out skin protection at the beach or poolside (a local manufacturer may be willing to donate sample sizes of sunscreen).

• Be ready to help in community emergencies. During major events with heavy attendance or those with a potential of health risk, such as a marathon race, provide a hospital-sponsored first-aid station.

Be ready to help in community emergencies.

TEN

ELEVEN

THE MEDIA INFORMED

Media relations:

• Keep the media informed about how the hospital is responding to pressing social problems, such as increases in the number of homeless, "crack" and boarder babies, and so on. Link these activities to increasing hospital costs.

• Publicize the hospital's provision of care for the poor, giving figures on numbers of patients served, types of services that are provided below cost, and/or total value of uncompensated care provided.

• Develop a generic paragraph to include in every news release you send out, emphasizing your hospital's social role. For "milestone" releases on the hospital's founding anniversary, National Hospital Week, and other annual occasions, develop a historically oriented release that emphasizes the evolution of your hospital toward an expanded social role.

• Recognize employees

• Identify ways your hospital serves the unique needs of a special population group — for example, by caring for miners suffering from black-lung disease in a coal-mining community. Use this as the basis for a feature story showing your hospital's community orientation.

• Put reporters on the mailing list to receive the hospital's annual report, community newsletter, and other publications. Add a personal note flagging story ideas for them.

• If the hospital's community contributions are an issue in your community, work with other hospitals in your area to develop economic-impact data showing how hospitals contribute to the economic life of the community as major employers and purchasers of goods and services. See the worksheet elsewhere in this kit for more information.

• Take advantage of community service time

RIGHT AT HOME

Positioning Your **Hospital** as a Community Resource

American Hospital Association

AHA

American Hospital Association Community Benefit Kit

Art Director: Mark Oldach
Designer: Don Emery
Fonts: Helvetica Condensed, Bodoni
The bold serif is used sparingly in headline copy, with the body copy set in a condensed sans serif. The retro illustrations, high contrast graphics, white space and graphic display type add visual appeal.

AGI digitimes TWO

Concept/Design: Rick Valicenti
Photography: Rick Valicenti, Tony Klassen
© 1991 AGI, Inc.
Fonts: Gill Sans Bold, Adobe Garamond

Roughly the size of compact disk packaging, this brochure promoting digipaks is produced on a kraft-like paper with a quilted cardboard cover. Four-color is printed on a glossy stock visible through die-cuts. The type treatment is progressive, using various styles, sizes and degrees of pitch. In this way, small bits of information are highlighted within running text.

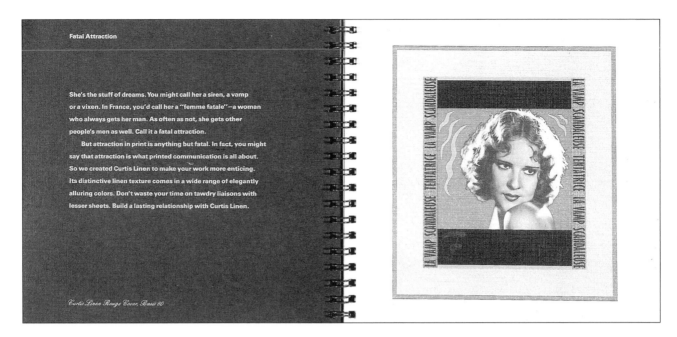

Fatal Attraction

She's the stuff of dreams. You might call her a siren, a vamp or a vixen. In France, you'd call her a "femme fatale"—a woman who always gets her man. As often as not, she gets other people's men as well. Call it a fatal attraction.

But attraction in print is anything but fatal. In fact, you might say that attraction is what printed communication is all about. So we created Curtis Linen to make your work more enticing. Its distinctive linen texture comes in a wide range of elegantly alluring colors. Don't waste your time on tawdry liaisons with lesser sheets. Build a lasting relationship with Curtis Linen.

Curtis Linen Rouge Cover, Basis 80

Creme de la Creme/Curtis Linen

Design: John Waters, Linda Gonsalves
© Waters Design Associates, Inc.
Fonts: Various

The Creme de la Creme brochure uses a tour theme to show off colored and textured stock by James River. The tour theme is carried out with a variety of display type, with the stock and weight information in an elegant script. The body type is a sans serif which is legible on a colored stock in a colored ink.

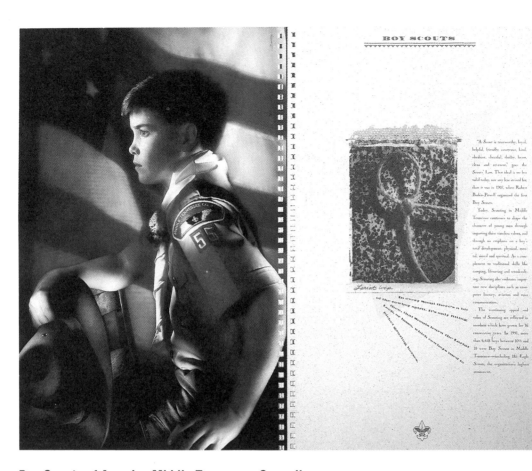

Boy Scouts of America Middle Tennessee Council

Concept and Design: Chuck Creasy

Typography: The Font Shop

© Chuck Creasy Creative 1990

Fonts: Madrone, Nicholas Cochin

Two faces with a lot of character work together in this annual report. The rough hewn serif body face has an old-fashioned quality, and the heavy square serif headline face holds up in warm colors on a tinted natural fiber sheet.

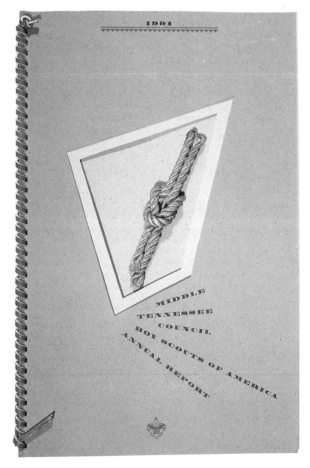

PARTY ALL THE WAY TO PARADISE

Three days out of Los Angeles and the social season is in high gear. Colorful cocktail parties in the Sky Room, in the Ritz Carlton, in private staterooms. Some you give. Some you go to. All in addition to the seemingly endless number of activities your cruise staff has planned for you. The fun and amusement are almost limitless. Overwhelming.

As one world cruiser put it, "Whatever you can think of that you personally would like to do today, I'll lay odds that you'll be able to do it . . ." Name your pleasure, name your hobby, name your fantasy. On the decks are walkers, joggers, readers, snoozers, sun worshippers. In the lounges there are people exercising gently, exercising strenuously. They're dancing. Learning about wine. About jewelry, about ice sculpture and carving vegetables into flowers. In the Lido there are crafts. And quizzes. And Scrabble. And checkers and backgammon and chess.

SOMETIMES THE BEST RECREATION OF ALL IS REFLECTING ON YESTERDAY'S ADVENTURES, DREAMING OF TOMORROW'S.

By the time you reach *Honolulu*, you'll be ready for a day at the beach, doing absolutely nothing. But will you be able to resist the lure of the island? The timeless beauty of Diamond Head. Pearl Harbor.

IN POLYNESIA BEAUTY IS EVERYWHERE, ESPECIALLY IN THE WARM OPEN SMILES OF THE PEOPLE.

The Pali. An evening shore excursion with ukulele-strumming singers and hip-swinging hula dancers.

Across the equator lies *Apia, Western Samoa,* the rustic treasure island where Robert Louis Stevenson spent the last, but no doubt the best, four years of his life. "A beautiful place," he wrote in his diary, "green forever . . . perfect shapes of men and women, with red flowers in their hair; nothing to do but study oratory and etiquette, sit in the sun and pick up the fruits as they fall . . ." There are also cascading waterfalls, fjord-like bays and quiet lagoons to see. And a *fiafia,* Samoa's version of a luau, to experience.

Under the light of a midnight moon, slip away for *Nuku'alofa, Tonga,* the last of the island kingdoms. Here, the royal family of Tonga, rulers for over a millennium, takes great pride in preserving the island's ancient Polynesian lineage. Natives still wear *valas,* dance the hypnotic *lakalaka,* and stage feasts of Tongan proportions — entree after entree . . . roast suckling pig, cray fish, chicken, octopus, pork and vegetables deliciously steamed in an underground oven (*umu*) and served on a long tray of plaited coconut fronds.

What a party! And yours to enjoy on a delightful shore excursion.

6

7

Holland America World Cruise

Art Director: John Hornall, Julie Tanagi-Lock
Designers: John Hornall, Julie Tanagi-Lock, Mary Hermes, Cynthia Pearce
Fonts: Weiss, Bauer Bodoni, Charlemagne, Futura Book, Ignatius, Matrix, Maximillian, Modula, Snell, Symbol, Totally Glyphic, Trajan, Zapf Dingbats

A variety of display types are used to feature different locales in this brochure. Weiss, set both in uppercase and lowercase and in small caps, has the right Old World romantic look that works for the whole piece.

esign

&

ABCDEFG

TYP

12345

M

Letterheads

Letterhead design poses some unique problems. Clients can be very sensitive about their identities, and may bring some irrational preferences to the table. They may insist on clinging to an out-of-date logo while asking for a completely new type treatment for the rest of the elements, for example. There are space constraints, and the card and letterhead must be functional. Letterhead is for sending messages, so clients should be able to type legible letters on the sheet. The address and phone number should be readable on a business card so potential customers can contact the business.

Despite these restrictions, letterhead projects are important and challenging. You help the client to project the right image, an image that is reinforced with every piece of business correspondence. Often the 2" x 3½" business card is all a potential client has for a contact. It must carry the right message both in form and content.

Type Considerations

Because of size constraints and the need to maintain legibility, subtle type decisions like weight, leading, kerning, the use of small caps and alignment make big statements.

The client and the market drive decisions about whether to use wit and humor for a light touch or to use classic, conservative faces and placement. Sometimes the company or the person's name will provide inspiration. A gimmick can be appropriate and help keep the company name in the mind of the customer, as long as it is not inconsistent with the image the client wants to portray.

Clean, Simple

This clean, simple approach to a letterhead for a large city hospital combines the italic versions of both a serif and a sans serif. Ample space is provided for generously leaded copy listing departments, divisions or specialties. This approach works well if there is an existing logo with a simple graphic with which to work.

The large, blocky *M* and its bars demand a strong, dark sans serif for the hospital's name. The slight slant of the Helvetica Condensed Black Italic complements the left to right motion of the *M* and the layout. The italic serif, New Baskerville, adds warmth but keeps the graphic look with the narrow, choppy rhythm created by generous leading. The address and phone information has also been set in the Helvetica Condensed Black Italic to help it stand out from the long list of departments.

Letterhead Sheet

Logotype: Helvetica Condensed Black Italic 14/18
Departments/Divisions: New Baskerville Italic 10/22
Address and Phone: Helvetica Condensed Black Italic 7/22

Envelope

Logotype: Helvetica Condensed Black Italic 14/18
Address: New Baskerville Italic 10/22

Business Card

Logotype: Helvetica Condensed Black Italic 12/18
Address and Phone: New Baskerville Italic 10/18
Person's Name: Helvetica Condensed Black Italic 10/18
Department: Helvetica Condensed Italic 10/18

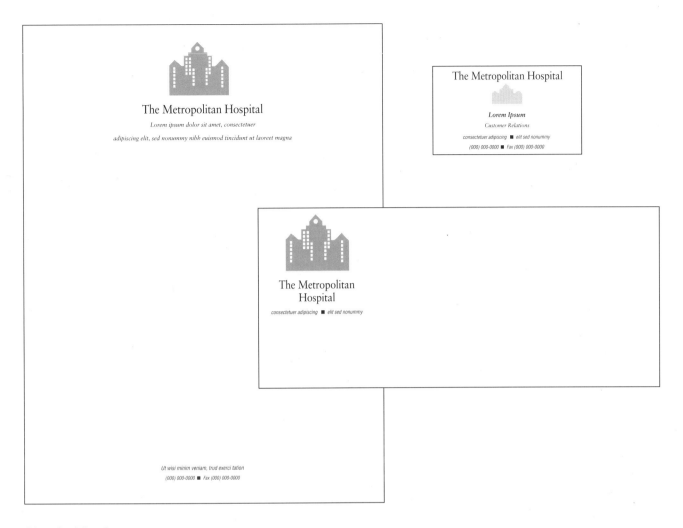

Classic, Timeless

A more traditional look for a city hospital is achieved with a dominant serif for the logotype and a centered orientation. The client's image suggests stability and inspires trust with a classic type design and layout. A small cap logo would work here, but it might look a little stodgy, especially if the small caps are applied to the rest of the copy.

Sabon combines an air of Victorian elegance with a liveliness created by its rather spiky serifs. The address and phone/fax information are set in a delicate sans serif so they are easily seen but don't overpower the Sabon. The slogan doesn't appear on the envelope, because that much copy would make the envelope look clunky and tilted to that side.

Letterhead Sheet

Logotype: Sabon 20/18, horizontal scaling: 90%
Slogan: Sabon Italic 10/22, centered
Address: Helvetica Condensed Italic 9/22
Phone: Helvetica Condensed Italic 8/16

Envelope

Logotype: Sabon 18/20, horizontal scaling: 90%
Address: Helvetica Condensed Italic 8/20

Business Card

Logotype: Sabon 20/18, horizontal scaling: 90%
Name: Sabon Bold Italic 11/22, centered
Department: Sabon Italic 9/22, centered

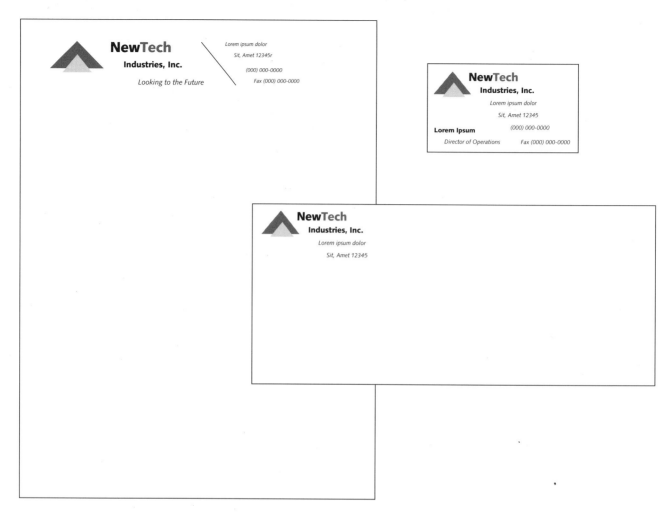

Geometric, Dynamic

This nontraditional, but simple, letterhead design works well for this start-up company that manufactures cutting-edge components they plan to market to manufacturers of home products. The nontraditional placement of the type on a staggered left margin reinforces the pyramidal shape of the logo.

Syntax has a little more flair than Helvetica, which tends to look more static and cerebral. Here, various weights of Syntax and use of the italic give the letterhead a "forward looking" feeling. The vigor and authority of the black weight is nicely balanced by the light, almost delicate looking italic. The striking contrast between these two weights is helpful in separating the different pieces of information on the business card.

Letterhead Sheet

Logotype: Syntax Black 20 pt. and 14 pt., and Syntax 20 pt., manual line spacing
Slogan: Syntax Italic 12 pt., manual line spacing
Address: Syntax Italic 10 pt., manual line spacing
Phone: Syntax Italic 10 pt., manual line spacing
Fax: Syntax Italic 10 pt., manual line spacing

Envelope

Logotype: Syntax Black 20 pt. and 14 pt., and Syntax 20 pt., manual line spacing
Address: Syntax Italic 10 pt., manual line spacing

Business Card

Logotype: Syntax Black 20 pt. and 14 pt., and Syntax 20 pt., manual line spacing
Address: Syntax Italic 10 pt., manual line spacing
Phone: Syntax Italic 10 pt., manual line spacing
Fax: Syntax Italic 10 pt., manual line spacing
Name: Syntax Black 10 pt.
Department/Division: Syntax Italic 10 pt., manual line spacing

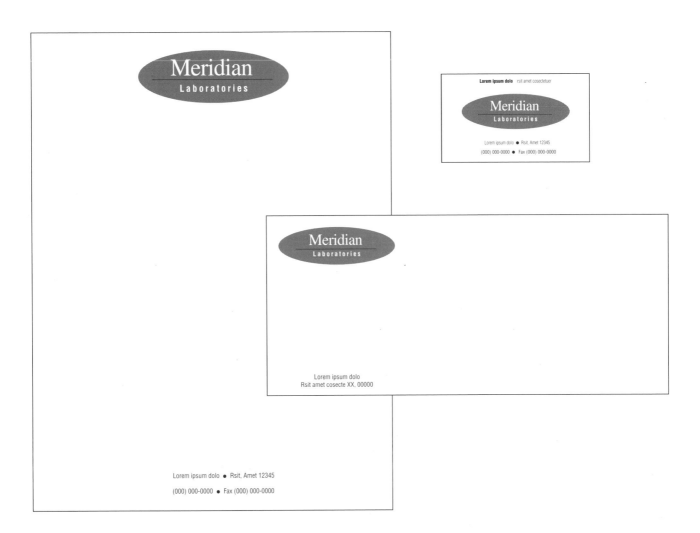

Warmth & Integrity

The mix of serif and sans serif logotype reversed out of an oval strikes a nice balance for a company that makes a medical product for consumers. The oval plate and the round bullets with the serif in the logo are warm and traditional (as in "our family of products").

Both Times Roman and Century Schoolbook have an old-fashioned, family look, but the association of Times with journalism and legal documents gives it more authority and integrity. And those qualities are as important as warmth for this client. Helvetica Condensed is used here because it is less horsy looking than Helvetica, but it still has the effective presence needed to make sure it is seen despite being quite small (only 10 pt.) and surrounded by white space. To save space the name and department are set on a single line on the business card, using the weight change to differentiate the information.

Letterhead Sheet

Logotype: Times Roman 36 pt. and Helvetica Bold Condensed 14 pt., *Laboratories* is set 26 points below *Meridian* measured baseline to baseline
Address and Phone: Helvetica Condensed 10/18

Envelope

Logotype: Times Roman 36 pt. and Helvetica Bold Condensed 14 pt., *Laboratories* is set 17 points below *Meridian* measured baseline to baseline
Address: Helvetica Condensed 10/12

Business Card

Person's Name and Title: Helvetica Black Condensed 10/18
Logotype: Times Roman 36 pt. and Helvetica Bold Condensed 14 pt., *Laboratories* is set 18 points below *Meridian* measured baseline to baseline
Address and Phone: Helvetica Condensed 10/18, address line is set 29 points up from the bottom of the card

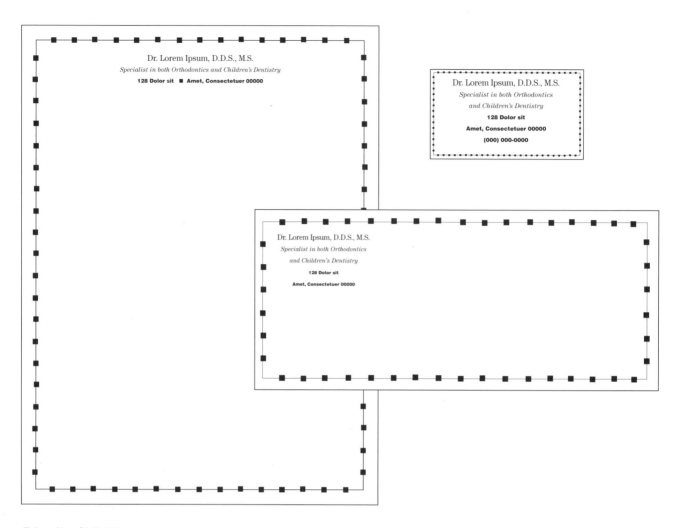

Friendly, Childlike

For an orthodontist who specializes in working with children, Century is the perfect face. It is round and open with a large x-height, and has a "See Spot run" quality. It mixes well with a heavy weight of Helvetica, also a very basic face with a slightly rounded, open look. Using Century Italic for the tagline sets it off from both logotype and address information without giving it undue emphasis. The centered typography is a classic arrangement for a letterhead system, but here it actually looks rather lively because the border pulls the eye quickly across the lines of type. The copy on the envelope is downsized for balance on the smaller surface.

Letterhead Sheet

Logotype: Century 14/18, centered
Tagline: Century Italic 11/18, centered
Address: Helvetica Black 9/18, centered
Phone Number: Helvetica Black 9/18, centered

Envelope

Logotype: Century 12/18, centered
Tagline: Century Italic 10/18, centered
Address: Helvetica Black 7/18, centered

Business Card

Logotype: Century 14/18, centered
Tagline: Century Italic 11/18, centered
Address and Phone: Helvetica Black 9/18, centered

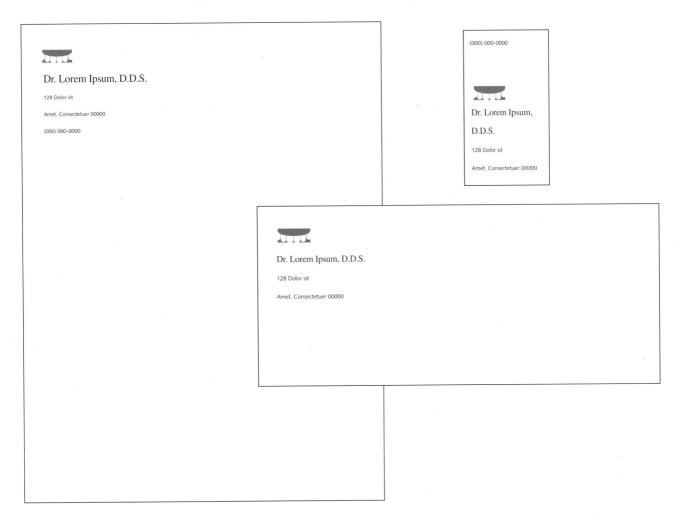

Fun, But Not Silly

A design with a lighthearted graphic of teeth needs a subdued type approach. The objective is be friendly, even fun looking, but the approach must not make the client appear silly. All type is set flush left under the logo and generously leaded for a clean, contemporary feel. Times Roman is a basic, neutral face, while the Syntax is light yet clear enough to be easily read. The tightly tracked Times adds a little dignity.

Note that the logotype is set in smaller type on the envelope and the business card so it will fit the proportions of the piece better. The type for the address information is small enough that it will fit all three pieces without adjustment. Even though the size of the logotype changes, the leading is kept constant to maintain the same vertical proportions in the column of type.

Letterhead Sheet
Logotype: Times Roman 18/28
Address and Phone: Syntax 9/28

Envelope
Logotype: Times Roman 14/28
Address: Syntax 9/28

Business Card
Phone: Syntax 9/28, baseline set 27 points from top edge of card
Logotype: Times Roman 14/18
Address: Syntax 9/28

Sophisticated, Dynamic

A high contrast, sophisticated look is right for an art gallery that is part of and shares a name with a retail development. The little squares are gradated for a shimmering quality and are reminiscent of windows in high-rise buildings. The square reinforces the name of the development, MidTown Square. This dynamic look relates to other elements of retail design such as signage, ads and tags by being angled like a stamp.

A condensed Bauer Bodoni works well for communicating sophistication and "city center." Helvetica Black has a cool, cerebral look that fits the image of the piece. Because it's a very sturdy face, it holds up well when reversed out of black or other dark colors even though it's set quite small, only 7 point.

Letterhead Sheet

Logotype: Bauer Bodoni 18 pt., horizontal scaling: 70%
Address, Phone and Fax: Helvetica Black 7/14
Graphic between lines of type is a Zapf Dingbat 7/14

Envelope

Logotype: Bauer Bodoni 20 pt., horizontal scaling: 70%
Address: Helvetica Black 7/14
Graphic above and below address is a Zapf Dingbat 7/14

Business Card

Logotype: Bauer Bodoni 20 pt., horizontal scaling: 70%
Address, Phone and Fax: Helvetica Black 7/14, first line is 20 points below the logotype measured baseline to baseline
Graphic between lines of type is a Zapf Dingbat 7/14
Name and Title: Bauer Bodoni 10/12

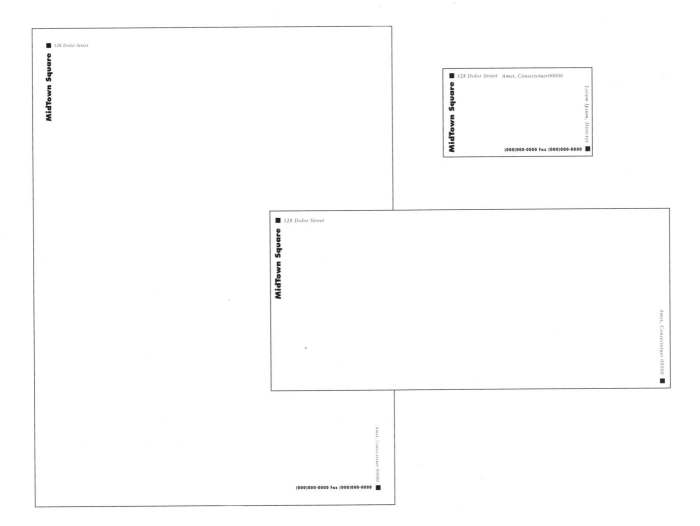

Artistic, Sophisticated

Corporate, yet still very graphic, this letterhead defines two corners of the "square" with type. This approach is restrained, but surprises with the placement of the logotype, which is usually parallel to the top edge. The minimalist approach and the unorthodox layout give it an artsy, sophisticated look. This type of design is appropriate for a gallery specializing in modern art; it has less retail, consumer appeal.

The very calligraphic letterforms of the Sabon Italic have an artistic, sophisticated feeling. It plays well against the intellectual, geometric letters of the Futura Extra Bold. There is also a dynamic contrast in the color of the type in the play of dark and light.

Letterhead Sheet

Logotype: Futura Extra Bold 12 pt., manual placement
Address, First Line: Sabon Italic 7 pt., manual placement
Address, Second Line: Sabon Italic 7 pt., manual placement
Phone and Fax: Futura Extra Bold 7 pt., manual placement

Envelope

Logotype: Futura Extra Bold 12 pt., manual placement
Address, First Line: Sabon Italic 8 pt., manual placement
Address, Second Line: Sabon Italic 8 pt., manual placement

Business Card

Logotype: Futura Extra Bold 12 pt., manual placement
Address: Sabon Italic 7 pt., manual placement
Name and Title: Sabon Italic 7 pt., manual placement
Phone and Fax: Futura Extra Bold 7 pt., manual placement

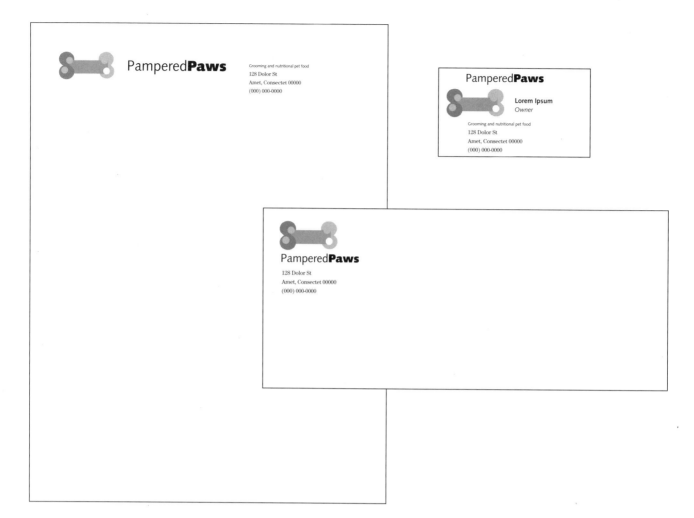

Clean, Friendly

A clean but friendly mix of faces works for this pet store, which emphasizes food and other supplies for the health and grooming of pets. There is a naive quality to the curved letterforms in Syntax that works well with the graphic bone logo. Century is also a simple, friendly serif. Since nutrition and health care (albeit pet health care) suggest an approach that inspires confidence, the size and placement of the type is precise and ordered rather than busy and cluttered.

The change in the weight of the type signals the word change; no space is left between the words because none is needed. Aligning a key line of type with the graphic on each piece in the system pulls the layout tightly together. The alignment is especially complex on the business card where the type is set so the descender on the lowercase *p* in *pampered* tucks inside the curve of the bone.

Letterhead Sheet

Logotype: Syntax and Syntax Ultra Black 24 pt., manual placement
Tagline: Syntax 7/14
Address: Century 9/14
Phone: Century 9/14

Envelope

Logotype: Syntax and Syntax Ultra Black 18 pt.
Address and Phone: Century 9/14

Business Card

Logotype: Syntax and Syntax Ultra Black 18 pt.
Name: Syntax Ultra Black 11/14
Title: Syntax Italic 10/14, manual placement
Tagline: Syntax 7/14
Address and Phone: Century 9/14

Pet "Beauty Salon"

This pet boutique emphasizes its grooming service, so the look borrows from the approach frequently used for beauty salons. There's a random quality to the pattern of paw prints, and the type placement varies from piece to piece. The tagline is set quite small and placed so it contrasts with the large, elaborate letterforms of the logo. The right aligned type on the business card solves the problem of fitting a large amount of copy in a small space without making the card look cluttered.

Optima in small caps is very elegant, so it works well for a tongue-in-cheek, boutique look. Palatino Italic, which can make almost any copy beautiful and rather glamorous, helps carry through the beauty salon look. Palatino and Optima usually look good together, since they are both rather light faces with letterforms that have a hand-drawn quality.

Letterhead

Logotype: Palatino Italic 24/30, horizontal scaling: 90%
Tagline: Optima small caps 7/16
Address and Phone: Optima small caps 9/16

Envelope

Logotype: Palatino Italic 24/30, horizontal scaling: 90%
Address: Optima small caps 9/16, baseline set 21 points below graphic

Business Card

Logotype: Palatino Italic 24/30, horizontal scaling: 90%
Name and Title: Optima small caps 9/16
Address and Phone: Optima small caps 9/16
Tagline: Optima small caps 7/16

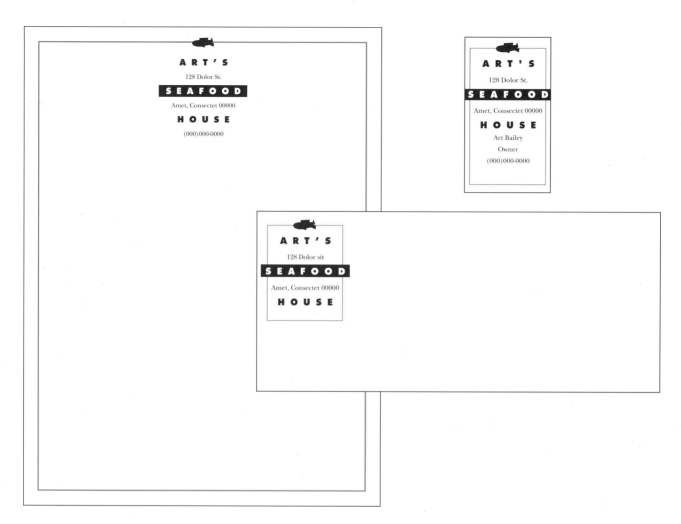

Nautical Look

Here the letterhead and card use bold, simple type. The eye is drawn to the word *seafood* because it is reversed out of a heavy bar. (Note that the bar is allowed to bleed only on the business card where it will be relatively simple to trim.) The emphasis is the same as it might be on a simple sign in front of the restaurant.

The lines of the heavy sans serif logo alternate with the lines of the address and phone number set in a delicate serif. The strong contrast in typeface and type color make it easier to read the information in the correct sequence. The generous spacing between the letters of the all caps logotype adds a little sophistication. The round capital *O*s of the Futura Extra Bold suggest portholes, adding to the nautical quality of the design. The vigor of the Futura Extra Bold is matched by the New Baskerville. This redesign of a venerable typeface has a very "alive" quality and stays legible under even adverse conditions.

Letterhead Sheet
Logotype: Futura Extra Bold caps 14/16, tracking: +14
Address and Phone: New Baskerville 11/13

Envelope
Logotype: Futura Extra Bold caps 14/24, tracking: +14
Address: New Baskerville 11/24

Business Card
Logotype: Futura Extra Bold caps 14/24, tracking: +14
Address: New Baskerville 11/24
Name, Title, Phone: New Baskerville 11/18

A R T ' S S E A F O O D B A R & G R I L L

128 DOLOR SIT AMET, CONSECTET 00000

(000) 000-0000

ART BAILEY, OWNER   (000) 000-0000

A R T ' S S E A F O O D

B A R & G R I L L

128 DOLOR   SIT AMET, CONSECTET 00000

A R T ' S S E A F O O D

B A R & G R I L L

128 DOLOR

SIT AMET, CONSECTET 00000

A "Homey Pub" Look

A traditional, "homey pub" approach to letterhead works well for a family restaurant that wants a slightly upscale look. The effect is achieved with caps in Goudy and the heavily tracked and leaded address copy, which is reminiscent of old, hot metal type. A graphic based on an architectural detail, some old tile work, is employed to communicate the traditional or Old World atmosphere.

The effect of small caps is created on the letterhead by altering the point size of the Goudy caps. On the other pieces where the type is smaller and the vertical spacing tighter, the Goudy is simply set all caps. The slightly flared serifs and the graceful letterforms draw the eye smoothly through the heavily tracked, all caps type, even though the line length is a bit longer than is usually comfortable for reading.

Letterhead Sheet

Logotype: Goudy caps, initial letters set 24/30, rest of letters set 18/30, horizontal scaling: 90%, tracking: +14
Address and Phone: Helvetica Condensed caps 9/30, tracking: +64

Envelope

Logotype: Goudy caps, 16/30, horizontal scaling: 90%, tracking: +14
Address: Helvetica Condensed caps 7/30, tracking: +64

Business Card

Name and Title: Helvetica Condensed caps 7/30, tracking: +64
Logotype: Goudy caps 16/30, horizontal scaling: 90%, tracking: +14
Address: Helvetica Condensed caps 7/30, tracking: +64

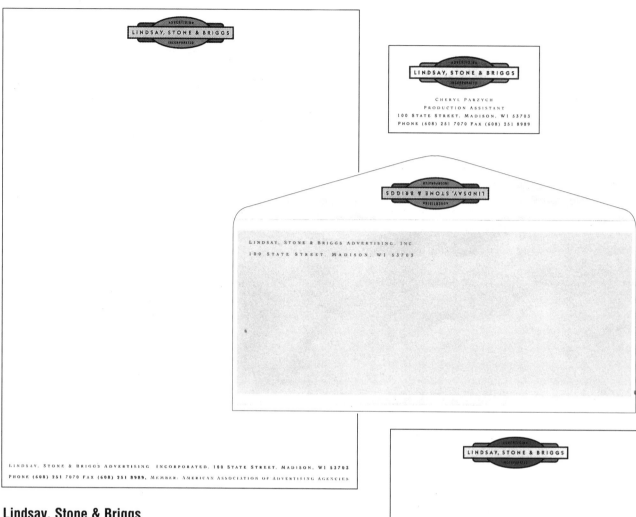

Lindsay, Stone & Briggs

Client: Lindsay, Stone & Briggs
Art Direction/Design: Kevin Wade, Dana Lytle
Fonts: Kabel, Helvetica, Sabon
Two sans serifs are combined on a logo with a strong deco look. The copy is all set in the serif in small caps. The generous tracking and wide line spacing are modern touches that still fit the overall geometric look.

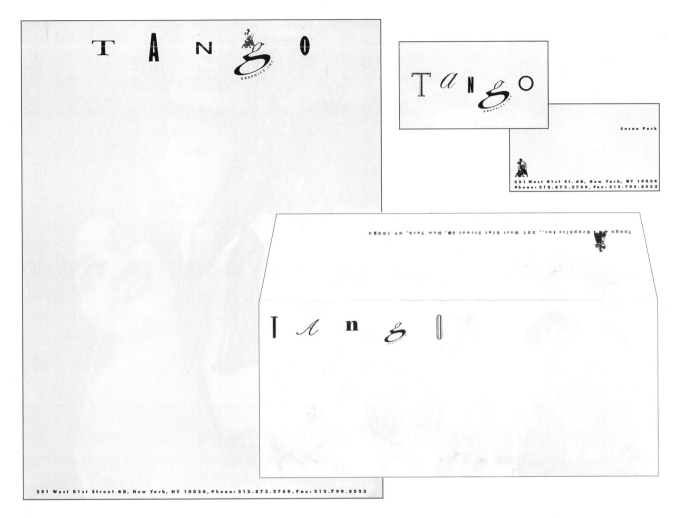

Tango

Client: Tango Graphics
Studio: Tango Graphics
Art Directors: Susan Schneider, Susan Peck
Designers: Susan Schneider, Susan Peck, Jennifer Patton, Hera Marashian
Fonts: Mixed Display Fonts
A distinctive "tango" of various typefaces in caps and uppercase and lowercase works well with the very graphic, retro icons. An illustration of tango dancers with a Rudolph Valentino look was printed in a light tint to create a subtle background.

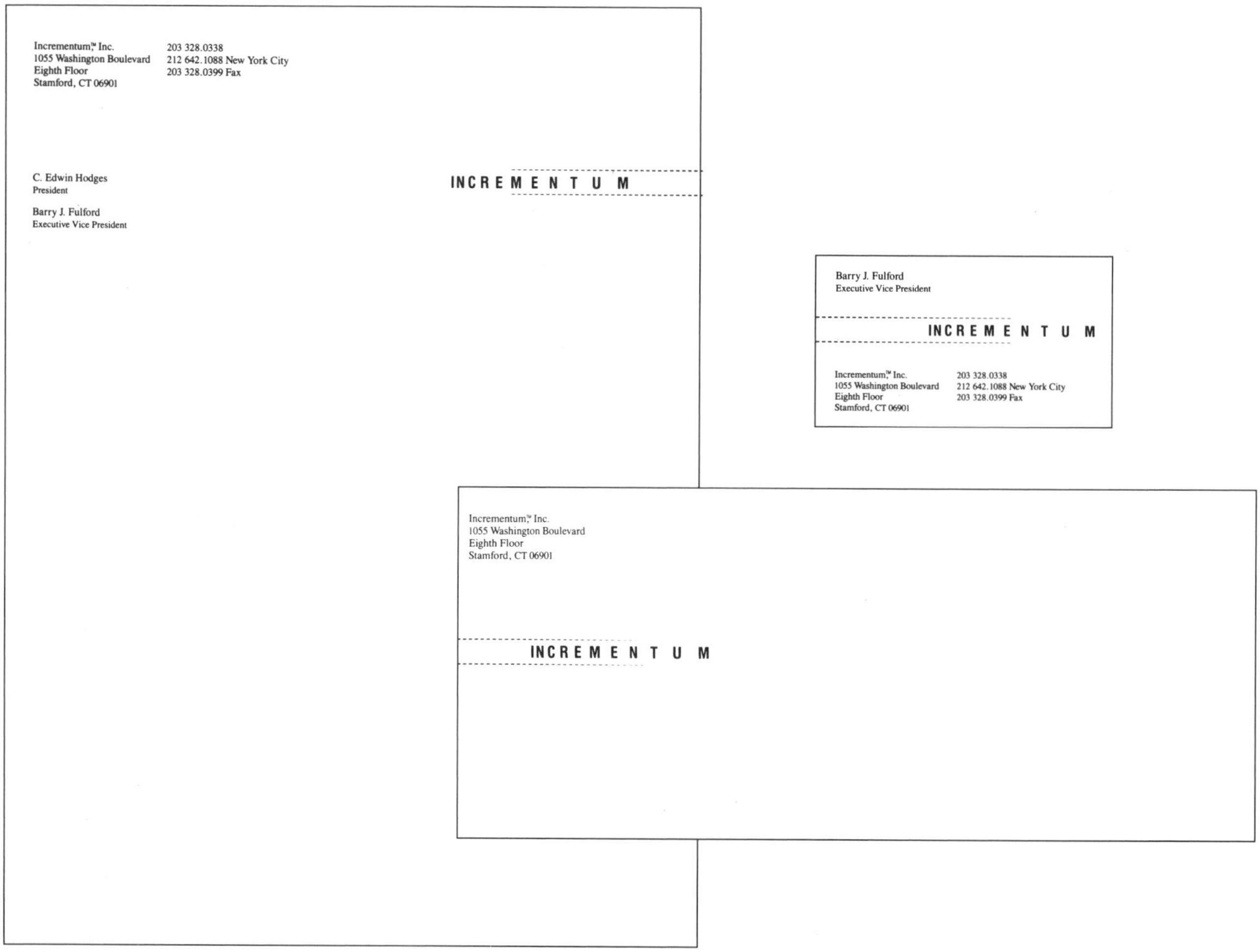

Incrementum™ Inc.   203 328.0338
1055 Washington Boulevard 212 642.1088 New York City
Eighth Floor   203 328.0399 Fax
Stamford, CT 06901

C. Edwin Hodges
President

Barry J. Fulford
Executive Vice President

INCREMENTUM

Barry J. Fulford
Executive Vice President

INCREMENTUM

Incrementum™ Inc.   203 328.0338
1055 Washington Boulevard 212 642.1088 New York City
Eighth Floor   203 328.0399 Fax
Stamford, CT 06901

Incrementum™ Inc.
1055 Washington Boulevard
Eighth Floor
Stamford, CT 06901

INCREMENTUM

Incrementum

Client: Incrementum
Art Director: Richard Danne
Designer: Richard Danne
Fonts: Helvetica Bold Condensed, Times Roman
Incrementum is an executive out-placement firm. The word
"incrementum" means growth, and the design is meant to
show passage and movement (from one job to another). A
professional, yet distinctive approach.

Italia

Client: Italia
Art Director: Jack Anderson
Designers: Jack Anderson, Julia LaPine
Fonts: Modern, Bodoni Italic
This retail look for a restaurant is created with Bodoni Italic and an illustration done in a loose style. The client's name is set in Modern. There's a family look to the variety of other applications created for the same client, including labels and T-shirts.

DuVerre

Client: DuVerre Glass, Ltd.

Art Director: Diti Katona, John Pylypczak

Designer: Diti Katona

Photo: Chris Nicholls

Fonts: Kunstler Script, Bodoni

An elegant, sophisticated look reminiscent of '40s typography for a store that carries upscale merchandise, including not only fine glass but also tableware and housewares.

Loyola Gallery

Client: Loyola Gallery Downtown

Designer: Tom Varisco

Fonts: Futura, Hand Lettering

A festive approach with Hand Lettering and Futura set on a
curve to complement the highly stylized script.

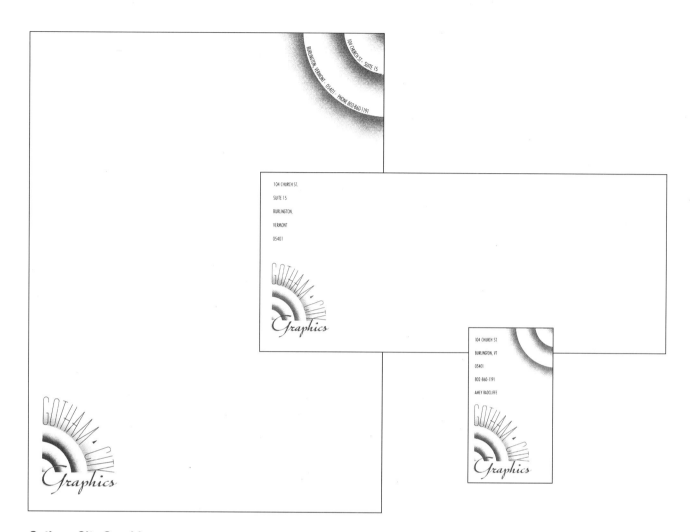

Gotham City Graphics

Client: Gotham City Graphics

Art Directors: Amey Radcliffe, Stephanie Salmon, Kathy Yanulavich

Fonts: Huxley Vertical, Trafton Script, Futura Italic Condensed

The period script face and the ultra condensed sans serif, both popular type approaches in the '20s and '30s, carry out the deco theme.

Comics Magazine Association of America, Inc.

355 Lexington Avenue, 17th Floor, New York, N.Y. 10017
(212) 661-4261 Fax (212) 370-9047

CMAA

Client: Marvel Entertainment Group, Inc.
Art Director: Clare Ultimo
Designer: Julie Hubner
Fonts: Hand Lettered, Bodoni Poster Compressed
A condensed bold Bodoni stands up in the bright fluores-
cent ink and complements the "WHAM! POW!" logotype
in the characteristic burst.

design & ABCDE M 1234 TY

Special Applications

This chapter includes a variety of print applications that you may have an opportunity to design. Each has its own special design constraints and opportunities.

Catalogs

The catalog can be a most effective mailer because the prospective customer perceives it as having value. This is especially true of magazine-style catalogs where four-color visuals are used lavishly. Often the recipient of a catalog has requested it or is on a small, targeted mailing list. It has a longer shelf life than a brochure and may be used frequently. For an industrial account such as a parts manufacturer, accuracy and organization are of primary importance.

Charts and Graphs

The size and weight of the type in an informational format like a chart must be consistent with the importance of the information. Layout should enhance the chart's usefulness. Typically, charts and graphs run with editorial copy; they provide information at a glance and also serve as illustrations that break up gray text. They should use the same palette of fonts as the editorial with the possible addition of a more graphic face.

Menus

The menu is part of a restaurant's identity. The type selections should be consistent with the mood established by the logo, other signage, decor, and the bill of fare. Other considerations are the clientele and the lighting in which the menu will be read. Be careful with translucent paper, small and delicate typography, and potentially distracting background elements if the menu must be read in dim light.

Calendars/Announcements

These pieces are often also sales tools meant to entice the recipient to attend events. There's often an obvious theme such as a season, holiday, party or sale. If the announcement is a listing of upcoming events, the look should reinforce the identity of the organization or be compatible with the mood of the events. Don't allow a calendar grid to dominate the information, and don't employ a rigid grid where announcement copy blocks may vary dramatically. If there's art, the type should recede. Graphics, large numerals and copy run sideways are all acceptable devices for this type of piece.

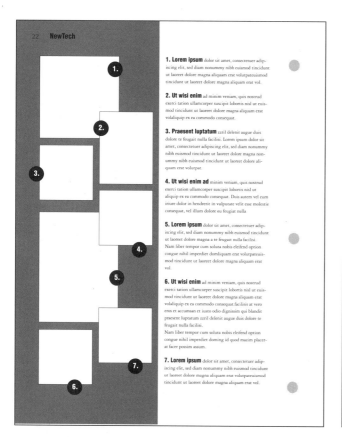

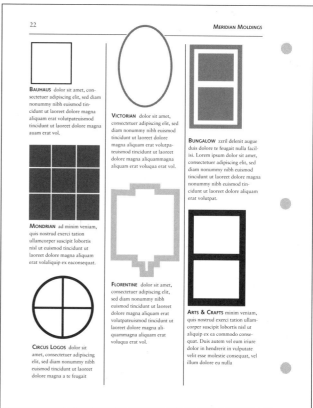

Practical & Attractive

This catalog for a company that manufactures electronic components illustrates a common problem in designing industrial catalogs. The product shots are a variety of in-plant photos, shot in a manufacturing environment; each subject is a different size. One way to organize the material and make an attractive layout is to group the photos in one column (or other section) and overlay them to make an interesting, effective arrangement. Use callouts to key each photo to its product information.

Condensed sans serifs are heavily used in product catalogs because they don't take up a lot of space and always have a clean look. Garamond is not quite as legible as Times Roman, but it has a fresh, contemporary look that is better suited to the product.

Product Name: Helvetica Black Condensed 12/14
Body Copy: Garamond 10/14
Number Callouts on Photos: Helvetica Black Condensed 14 pt.
Folio/Running Head: Helvetica Black Condensed 14 pt.

Product With Style

When the product is shown in line drawings or simple, high contrast photos and the sell copy needs to run with the illustration, a three-column grid offers more variety. The copy at the bottoms of the columns is not perfectly aligned, so the page looks friendlier and more active. For an elegant product such as moldings or frames, small caps add a touch of class to the headings.

Syntax and Sabon both convey a feeling of style and fashion that suits this type of product. These faces are also quite practical as well. They have slightly condensed proportions that help them fit into the rather narrow columns without many bad line breaks. But do note that both space a little open and should be allowed to do so at this text size.

Product Name: Syntax Bold small caps 12/14
Body Copy: Sabon 10/14
Folio/Running Head: Syntax Bold small caps 12/14

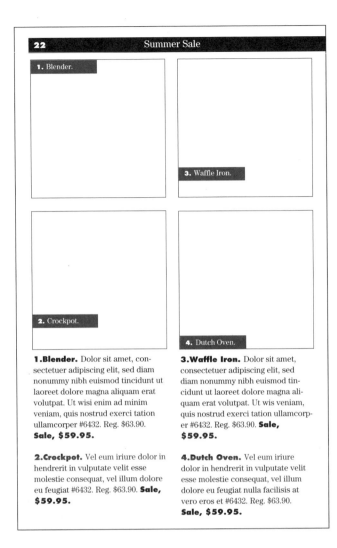

1. Blender.

3. Waffle Iron.

2. Crockpot.

4. Dutch Oven.

1.Blender. Dolor sit amet, consectetuer adipiscing elit, sed diam nonummy nibh euismod tincidunt ut laoreet dolore magna aliquam erat volutpat. Ut wisi enim ad minim veniam, quis nostrud exerci tation ullamcorper #6432. Reg. $63.90. **Sale, $59.95.**

2.Crockpot. Vel eum iriure dolor in hendrerit in vulputate velit esse molestie consequat, vel illum dolore eu feugiat #6432. Reg. $63.90. **Sale, $59.95.**

3.Waffle Iron. Dolor sit amet, consectetuer adipiscing elit, sed diam nonummy nibh euismod tincidunt ut laoreet dolore magna aliquam erat volutpat. Ut wis veniam, quis nostrud exerci tation ullamcorper #6432. Reg. $63.90. **Sale, $59.95.**

4.Dutch Oven. Vel eum iriure dolor in hendrerit in vulputate velit esse molestie consequat, vel illum dolore eu feugiat nulla facilisis at vero eros et #6432. Reg. $63.90. **Sale, $59.95.**

Men's Shirts
Dolor sit amet, consectetuer adipiscing elit, sed diam nonummy nibh euismod tincidunt ut laoreet dolore magna aliquam erat volutpat. Ut wis veniam, quis nostrud exerci tation ullamcorper #6432. Reg. $43.90. **Sale, $39.95.**

Turtleneck.
Vel eum iriure dolor in hendrerit in vulputate velit esse molestie co sequat, vel illum dolore eu feugiat nulla facilisis at vero eros et #6432. Reg. $43.90. **Sale, $39.95.**

NEW!

Wool Slacks
Dolor sit amet, consectetuer adipiscing elit, sed diam nonummy nibh euismod tincidunt ut laoreet dolore est magna aliquam erat etto volutpat. Ut wis veniam, quis nostrud exerci tation ullamcorperUt wis veniam, quis ntrudUt wis veniam, s nostrud Ut veniam, quis nostrud #6432. Reg. $43.90. **Sale, $49.95.**

NEW!

Riding Boots. Vel eum iriure dolor in hendrerit in vulputate velit esse moles tie consequat, vel illum dolore eu feugiat nulla facilisis atque vero eros et vel illum dolore eu feugiat nulla vel illum neq dolore eu feugiat nulla vel illum dolore eu feugiatnulla #6432. Reg. $43.90. **Sale, $39.95.**

To order call
1-800-000-0000

Clean, Geometric

This is a clean, contemporary approach to a catalog of housewares. Each photo features a single product with a simple, attractive background. The labels on the photos have been placed so they don't interfere with the product. The black bar is a unifying graphic element for a clean, geometric approach.

Century and Futura Extra Bold are clean and legible typefaces. Because the product photos are the focus of the strongly geometric layout, no type is angled or set in circles, starbursts or other violator devices. The Futura Extra Bold so dominates the Century that it can be reduced by a point size and still have extra emphasis.

Product Name and Sale Price: Futura Extra Bold 9/13
Body Copy: Century 10/13
Labels on Photos: Futura Extra Bold 9 pt. (numbers) and Century 9 pt. (product names)
Folio: Futura Extra Bold 9 pt.
Running Head: Century 9 pt.

Conservative, Quality

For this catalog of quality clothing, the copy wraps around the irregularly shaped outlines of the product shots. When there is a more complex wrap, read the copy carefully after it has been set to make sure that it has broken well and can be easily understood.

The Goudy is set much larger to emphasize the product names, and the sale prices are set in the bold weight to give them slightly more emphasis than the rest of the copy. The black, condensed sans serif is used sparingly for the violators and the toll-free number. The overall effect is conservative and projects an image of quality.

Product Name: Goudy 18/24
Body Copy: Goudy 10/13
Sale Price: Goudy Bold 9/13
Folio: Helvetica Black Condensed 12 pt.
Running Head: Goudy Bold 14 pt.
Call to Action: Goudy 10/12
Toll-Free Number: Helvetica Black Condensed 12/14
Violators: Helvetica Black Condensed caps 12 pt.

THE CORNER DELI

128 E 4TH STREET

🙠 🙠 SOUPS 🙠 🙠

Clam Chowder 2.75
    consectetuer adipiscing elit
French Onion 3.25
    tincidunt ut laoreet dolore
Garden Vegetable 1.75
    Ut wisi enim ad minim v
The Daily Special 1.75
    ullamcorper suscipit lobortis
    nisl ut aliquip ex ea commodo
    consequat.

🙠 🙠 SANDWICHES 🙠 🙠

Tem vel eum iriure dolor in hen-
drerit in vulputate velit esse mol
estie consequat.
Ham. 5.25
Corned Beef. 5.25
Pastrami. 5.25
Turkey Breast. 5.25
Roast Beef. 5.25
Grilled Cheese. 3.25
    (Swiss, American, Cheddar)

🙠 🙠 SALADS 🙠 🙠

French Chef. 4.25
Mexican Chef. 6.25
Beef Taco. 5.25
Chicken Taco. 5.25
Cobb Delight. 5.25
Shrimp Caesar. 6.25
Chicken Caesar 5.25
Steak Caesar. 5.25
    augue duis dolore te feugait nulla facil
    isi. Lorem ipsum dolor sit amet, con
    sectetuer adipiscing elit.

🙠 🙠 DESERTS 🙠 🙠

Fresh Baked Pies 1.75
    consectetuer adipsed diam
U-Make Sundae Bar 2.25
Hot Fudge Cake. 2.50

🙠 🙠 BEVERAGES 🙠 🙠

Cofee or Iced Tea 75
All Fountain Drinks. 1.50
    Special Sodas. 1.85

THE GARDEN SPOT

128 E 4TH STREET

SOUPS

French Onion
*sit amet, consectetuer adip-
iscing elit, sed diam nonummy nibh euismod tincidunt
ut laoreet dolore magna aliquam erat volutpat.*

Baked Potato
*enim ad minim veniam, quis
nostrud exerci tation ullamcorper suscipit lobortis
Nisl ut aliquip ex ea commodo consequat.*

Tomato Bisque
*vel eum iriure dolor in hen-
drerit in vulputate velit esse
molestie consequat, vel
illum dolore eu feugiat nulla
facilisis at ipso lorem est
vero eros et*

Minestrone
*iusto odio dignissim qui
blandit praesent luptatum
zzril delenit augue duis
dolore te feugait nulla facilisi.*

SALADS

Cobb Salad
*dolor sit amet, consectetuer
adipiscing elit, sed diam
nonummy nibh euismod
tincidunt ut laoreet dolore
ma*

BLT Salad
*enim ad minim veniam,
quis nostrud exerci tation
ullamcorper suscipit lobortis naliquip ex ea commodo
consequat.*

Chef Salad
*vel eum iriure dolor in hen-
drerit in vulputate velit esse
molestie consequat,*

Garden Spot
*at vero eros et accumsan et
iusto odio dignissim qui
blandit luptatum zzril
zzril delenit augue duis
dolore te feugait nulla facilisi.*

Side Salad
*tempor cum soluta nobis
eleifend option congue nihil
imperdiet doming id quod
mazim placerat facer pos-
sim assu*

SALADS FROM THE SEA

Shrimp Caesar
*sit amet, consectetuer adip-
iscing elit, sed diam nonummy nibh euismod tincidunt
ut laoreet dolore magna aliquam erat volutpat.*

Crab Deluxe
*enim ad minim veniam, quis
nostrud exerci tation ullamcorper suscipit lobortis
Nisl ut aliquip ex ea commodo consequat.*

Neptune's Garden
*vel eum iriure dolor in hen-
drerit in vulputate velit esse
molestie consequat, vel illum
dolore eu feugiat nulla facilisis at neque mini allo est
vero eros et*

Salade Niçoise
*iusto odio dignissim qui
blandit praesent luptatum
zzril delenit augue duis
dolore te feugait nulla facilisi.*

Old-Fashioned & Casual

The decorative flourishes and centered small caps have an old-fashioned yet casual quality. This look would work well for a deli or bar menu. The body copy is set large enough to be legible when printed on a tinted sheet, which would work well with the old-fashioned type treatment. Rather than reduce the type size when an explanation of an item is needed, a deep indent is used to clarify the levels of information. Although it looks small when compared to the body copy, the smallest type is still 14 points.

In order to fit the pairs of dingbats on either side of even the longest heading, Helvetica Condensed is used to increase the character-per-inch count without losing legibility. The black weight helps organize the information by clearly signaling which copy should be read first. Garamond's graceful lines offer a nice contrast to the hard-edged, geometric Helvetica Condensed.

Restaurant Name: Garamond small caps 48 pt.
Address: Garamond 18/30
Headings: Helvetica Black Condensed small caps with Zapf dingbats, both 28 pt., centered
Body Copy: Garamond 18/24
Additional Descriptive Copy: Garamond 14/14

Light, Sophisticated

The flush left format and ample white space give this menu a light, more sophisticated look. The names of the menu items are set off with both a weight change and spacing to prevent them from getting lost in the long copy. The prices are run into the copy and given no special emphasis.

Very generous pitch is used for the logotype so it appears centered across the top of the menu and fits well with the graphic and continues the light theme. Both the Palatino Bold and the Helvetica Bold Condensed are strong and legible enough to permit them to be printed in a color, even if a tinted sheet is used. Palatino has a naturally grace-ful, sophisticated quality, especially in the italic. The large amounts of white space soften the Helvetica Condensed so it is prominent but not overly assertive.

Restaurant Name: Helvetica Bold Condensed small caps 36 pt., manual letterspacing
Address: Helvetica Bold Condensed small caps 14/30, manual letterspacing
Headings: Helvetica Bold Condensed small caps 18/20
Item Name: Palatino Bold 12/14
Body Copy: Palatino Italic 12/14

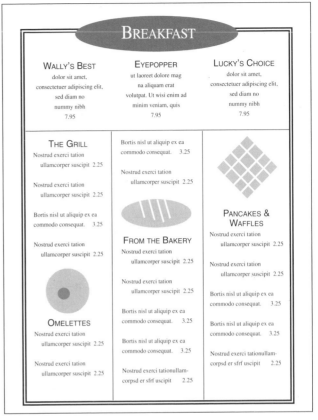

Formal, Elegant

A menu for a very formal restaurant should be understated. Narrow lines of centered copy and a tinted border are formal touches. You won't always have equal amounts of copy for each menu item, so you may have to modify your design slightly to accommodate unusually long or short items. Most of the items on this page have short descriptions, so they tuck nicely into shorter lines between the item names. The very long descriptions are still centered on the page, but the first line is allowed to extend beyond the item name and price for balance. The restaurant's name would appear on the outside cover of this multi-page menu.

New Baskerville Italic and Optima Italic are used to suggest the type on a formal invitation. Although a script face would actually be used on an invitation, an italic face gives the effect of script but is more legible.

Headings: New Baskerville Italic 28 pt.
Item Name and Price: Optima Italic small caps 18/20
Descriptions: New Baskerville Italic 14/20

Casual, Easily Updated

Many casual bistros and informal hotel restaurants use a single-page menu for each meal. These restaurants change their offerings frequently, so the menu must be easy to update. Since the specials are most likely to change, they are isolated at the top of the page rather than grouped with other items. This space could also be used for items carried over to another meal; many hotel and other casual restaurants may offer a few breakfast dishes at lunchtime, for example.

A light but sophisticated look is created with two standard typefaces when the Times and Helvetica are generously leaded. (Because these fonts are available on almost every printer, they are an especially good choice if you are selling the client a template that will be used to produce frequent updates.) The screened-back graphics add sophistication.

Name of Menu: Times Roman small caps 36 pt.
Headings and Specials: Helvetica small caps 18/19
Body Copy: Times Roman 12/19

Graphic, Lively

Here a 5½" x 8½" mailer has a clean, three-column listing of upcoming events. The boxes are for publicity photos. The numerals for the dates are set at a normal text size. With photos, it is unnecessary to use large numerals for visual interest.

The understated black-and-white play created by the condensed sans serif and the reversed, boxed type for the captions works well for a calendar of evening performances. Helvetica Extra Compressed creates clean breaks on the page without adding a lot of space between items. Garamond Italic is slightly darker than the roman and, therefore, a better match for the dramatic Helvetica Extra Compressed.

Headline: Helvetica Bold Condensed 24 pt. and Garamond 24 pt.
Dates and Titles of Events: Helvetica Extra Compressed 12/14
Body: Garamond Italic 11/13
Captions: Helvetica Extra Compressed 12/14

Friendly, Active

This 5½" x 8½" mailer lists classes, workshops and weekend activities. In the absence of photos, the large numerals set in an open serif add a decorative touch. The message is open and accessible. This approach would also work for a poster.

The Syntax Ultra Black subheads are a point size smaller than the body because their heavy weight dominates the body in the same size. It has been screened back slightly in the headline, so it won't dominate the Century there. The strong, chunky characters of Syntax are strongly contrasted with the round, flowing letterforms of the Century, giving the page a dynamic feeling without losing the friendliness projected by Century.

Headline: Syntax Ultra Black and Century 42 pt.
Dates: Century 24/30
Names of Events: Syntax Ultra Black 10/12
Body: Century Italic 11/14

"Back to School" Look

This 5½" x 8½" retail mailer for a series of fashion shows carries through the "Back to School" theme with the apple graphic. Lots of white space is balanced by a simple, centered, text format. This piece would be especially effective printed on a bright paper; for example, it could be printed on a bright red paper with a bright yellow ink surrounding the apple and a green for the leaf and stem.

Century is the ideal choice to carry out the theme in the headline type, since it evokes memories of school textbooks. Futura Extra Bold has round *O*s and a chunky geometric quality perfect for a program for children. But in the narrow format of the two-column listing, the compressed Helvetica is more readable.

Headline: Futura Extra Bold 36/60, centered, and Century 36/60, centered
Dates: Futura Extra Bold 14/45, tracking: +16, centered
Subheads: Helvetica Extra Compressed 12/14, centered
Body: Century Italic 12/14, centered

"High Fashion" Look

A more sophisticated fashion show announcement is handled with a very generously tracked bold sans serif and a tightly condensed serif. Using a condensed face for part of the headline reflects the tall, thin appearance of high fashion models, as does running the copy full frame top and bottom, with white space on the sides.

You don't always need a computer full of display fonts to create special effects. While the Times here is not a perfect substitute for fonts such as Modula or Industria, it creates a similar effect without the expense of a display font that you may not use again for months. The Futura Extra Bold set all caps isn't tracked as heavily as the Futura in the headline to create a change in weight and impact.

Headline: Futura Extra Bold 12/60, tracking: +90, and Times Roman 96/60, horizontal scaling: 50%
Date: Futura Extra Bold 12/36, tracking: +90
Store Hours: Times Roman Italic 12/36, horizontal scaling: 90%
Subheads: Futura Extra Bold caps 10/36, tracking: +20
Body: Times Roman Italic 10/36, horizontal scaling: 90%

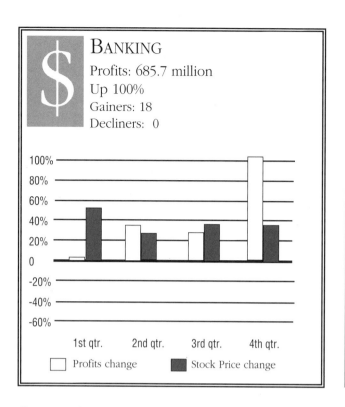

3rd Quarter Earnings			
Company	**Earnings (1,000s)**	**Earnings /share**	**Earnings change**
Bundle's	$678	$0.31	207%
Caty	-$3,900	$0.49	5%
Family Stuff	$10,937	$0.20	53%
Lil's	$678	$0.31	207%
Ollie's	-$3,900	$0.49	5%
Rudd's	$10,937	$0.20	53%
Ryder	$678	$0.31	207%
Safere	-$3,900	$0.49	5%
STVV	$10,937	$0.20	53%
TWW	$678	$0.31	207%
Vanguard	-$3,900	$0.49	5%
Wall's	$10,937	$0.20	53%

Conservative

A serif in small caps is an appropriate look for the heading of a chart for the banking industry. The subhead, however, was set in uppercase and lowercase both to make the copy more readable and to keep the chart from looking top-heavy. A small caps setting has considerably more weight and bulk. The double rule also has a "bank note" formality. Screens of gray are subdued and conservative; a graphic, black-and-white treatment would be too dramatic for this client.

Garamond is a formal, traditional face that is well suited for this conservative look. It has been slightly condensed to conserve space. Helvetica Condensed is a clean, dark face, and it holds up well in small sizes. The numerals are quite legible, a critical issue in chart design.

Head: Garamond small caps 18/20, horizontal scaling: 95%
Subhead: Garamond 12/14 and 11/13, horizontal scaling: 95%
Labels: Helvetica Condensed 9/16

Packed & Legible

When you have several charts in a magazine or a newspaper article, reversing the head out of a dark screen or a dark color allows the reader to find them easily. The numbers in this chart are legible enough to hold up over a light screen of black or a second color. (Although there are exceptions to every rule, specify that the tint be screened back to 10 percent in order to be sure that the type can easily be read.) When setting tables of numbers, proof carefully for correct decimal alignment before you print.

Times Roman is a relatively compact face, but it has been condensed an additional 5 percent in this chart packed with information. A serif face makes the names easier to read, especially if some are unfamiliar to the reader. In order to fit the long, precise labels in, the Helvetica Condensed was replaced with the highly compact Helvetica Compressed.

Head: Times Roman 22 pt.
Headings: Helvetica Compressed 11/12
Company Names: Times Roman 11/18, horizontal scaling: 95%
Numbers: Helvetica Condensed 10/18

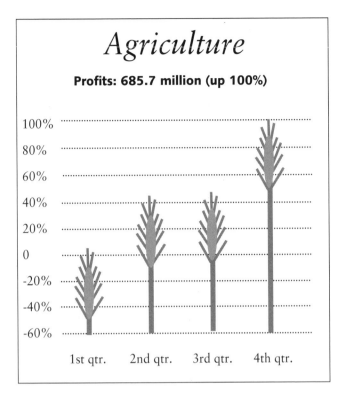

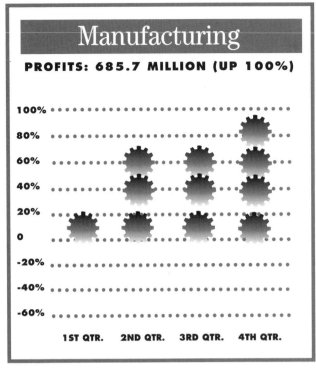

Light, Active

The graphics add a light touch to this simple chart. The italic head reinforces the informal mood. Because there is little copy, a light, attractive serif works wells for the labels. Note how much space the numerals occupy here compared to how much they have in the other graphs in this section. Even though the Sabon has been condensed 5 percent, the numerals and the percent signs are still much looser than the sans serifs.

Sabon adds interest without competing with the graphics. The strongly slanted serifs of the italic letterforms give the heading a feeling of motion. The Syntax Black subhead gives the heading a solid base and links it with the graph below. There's also a nice contrast between the open letterspacing of the heading and the more compact subhead.

Head: Sabon Italic 24 pt., horizontal scaling: 95%
Subhead: Syntax Black 10/12
Labels: Sabon 10/20, horizontal scaling: 95%

Bold, Geometric

The gear icons are bold and round, so a bolder weight of type is called for. Futura Extra Bold works well with the geometric shaped gears. The headline reversed out of the dark box and supported by the bold subhead has a lot of weight to balance this area against the rest of the graph.

Century is a nice, rounded face that complements the roundness of the gears. Its sturdy serifs hold up well when printed reversed. Futura Extra Bold also has rounded letterforms; even the zeros are circular. Be careful when printing this very heavy weight of Futura on a 300 dot-per-inch printer. The openings in the 4s are tiny and start to fill in when the type is small as it is here (7 point).

Head: Century 22/24, horizontal scaling: 95%
Subhead: Futura Extra Bold caps 9/11, tracking: +12
Labels: Futura Extra Bold 7/20

Downtown Binders

Art Director: Stan Evenson
Designer: Stan Evenson
Fonts: Various
A high contrast, festive typographic solution is used for binders. A sophisticated medley of serifs, sans serifs and calligraphy.

MVP CD Package

Art Director: Tommy Steele
Designer: Glenn Sakamoto
Fonts: Various
An updated, classic approach mixes fonts and simple
shapes, circles and squares with updated colors and tex-
tures.

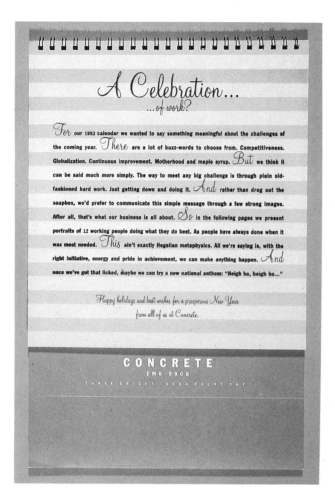

Concrete Calendar

Art Director: John Pylypczak, Diti Katona
Illustrator: Ross MacDonald
Fonts: Franklin Gothic, Script
A self-promotion piece for Concrete, the calendar uses a combination of a script and a sans serif face with '50s illustrations and color palette.

Food Services of America Calendar

Art Director: Jack Anderson
Designer: Jack Anderson, Mary Hermes
Photographer: Darrell Peterson
Fonts: Palatino, Garamond

Although this design uses traditional, classic type, the overall effect is very open and graphic. Old style numerals set at an extremely large size become powerful graphic elements. The formality of the Old style numerals and the classic serif face are offset by the large visuals with loose borders, the handwritten captions, and the generous white space.

Friend & Johnson Sourcebook

Designer: Bryan L. Peterson, Scott Paramski

Fonts: Various

A directory of photographers and illustrators with introductory copy about the state of graphic design, this book is distributed to art directors and graphic designers who create sophisticated layout and type design.

Financial Highlights

Northern Telecom has turned in a solid performance, the more remarkable for being achieved in a global economic downturn. Revenues from the integration of acquisition STC PLC strengthened the company's operations.

Revenues for 1991 were $8.18 billion, up 21 percent from $6.77 billion in 1990. Earnings per common share were $2.03, up 13 percent from $1.80 in 1990. Net earnings applicable to common shares for 1991 were $497 million, up 14 percent from $436 million in 1990.

Millions of dollars except per share figures	1991	1990	1989
Revenues	$8,182.5	$6,768.7	$6,105.5
Net earnings applicable to common shares	496.5	436.0	354.1
Net earnings per common share	2.03	1.80	1.47
Dividends per common share	.32	.30	.28
Common shareholders' equity	3,675.7	3,224.4	2,695.5
Working capital	172.3	1,236.7	1,024.1
Capital expenditures	514.0	441.7	369.5
Research and development and engineering expenses (gross)	1,231.6	1,029.4	927.0
Common shares outstanding (as at December 31, in millions)	245.6	243.5	241.9
Average common shares outstanding (in millions)	244.6	242.5	240.9
Common shareholders (as at December 31)	10,492	11,013	13,646
Employees (as at December 31)	57,059	49,039	47,572

All dollar amounts in this annual report are in U.S. dollars unless otherwise stated.

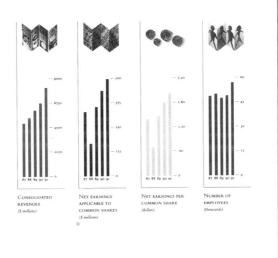

CONSOLIDATED REVENUES ($ millions)

NET EARNINGS APPLICABLE TO COMMON SHARES ($ millions)

NET EARNINGS PER COMMON SHARE (dollars)

NUMBER OF EMPLOYEES (thousands)

Northern Telecom

Art Director: John Pylypczak, Diti Katona
Designer: John Pylypczak
Illustrator: Doug Frazer, Valerie Sinclair
Fonts: Bembo, Franklin Gothic

The chart and graphs shown here are typical of those included in annual reports. The serif face used for the editorial copy is repeated in both figures. The setting is simple and clean; even tiny type used for the labels on the four graphs is quite legible.

Q

TUVWXYZ

123456

design

m7

Using Display Type

Display type can create or enhance the mood of your print work. It helps create a unique identity in a masthead, headline, logo, or on a book jacket. Choose a display face because it is right for the project, not just because you like it or it's trendy. Old woodcut faces would be effective in an ad with an old-fashioned theme, but a bitmapped or futuristic face would work better on a computer firm's letterhead.

There are a wide range of display types, some more legible than others. But, generally speaking, display type should be confined to short pull quotes, mastheads, logos, initial caps and short headlines. It's easy to overuse display type. The average reader won't wade through a lengthy headline in a script or an ultra condensed or ultra expanded face. Display faces are meant to attract attention. Use a display face too often, and you'll have so much emphasis on the page that readers won't be able to decide what information is important.

If you're creating a piece for a highly visual or design literate audience, you can use more display type. You can also use less readable type because this audience will work at figuring out the message. When the information being presented isn't important, layering display type in weights and colors can create a textural background.

NIBH EUISMOD TINCIDUNT UT LAOREET DOLORE
MAGNA ALIQUAM ERAT VOLUTPAT.

Fluid, Light

This newsletter would work for a radio station that features jazz, classical or easy listening music. The rolling script says lighter than air. Scripts are fluid faces that communicate a sense of fluid motion such as a ballet, or a floating quality suitable for jazz or classical music. Scripts work well with carefully placed, very heavy faces as anchors. The masthead suggests a piece of sheet music with the bursts of script on the horizontal lines of an elongated sans serif.

Although scripts are quite beautiful, they shouldn't be used to set more than a dozen short lines of copy. This design, therefore, adds a third face for the body copy and confines the script face to display type. Garamond has a quiet grace and elegance that make it a good fit with the overall look of the piece. The Futura has personality and a distinction, but it is not flamboyant. It supports rather than competes with the script face.

Masthead: Embassy 154 pt. (*Air*) and Futura Extra Bold caps 12 pt., horizontal scaling: 150%

Publication Information: Futura Extra Bold 7/34, tracking: +30

Table of Contents Numbers: Futura Extra Bold 24/26, horizontal scaling: 150%

Table of Contents Copy: Garamond 14/24

Heads: Futura Extra Bold caps 12 pt., horizontal scaling: 150%

Initial Cap: Embassy 60 pt.

Body: Garamond 12/15

Pull Quote: Embassy 24/24

Caption: Futura caps 7/15

Bold, Graphic

This newsletter for a contemporary music station has an irregular grid and strong, high-contrast type. The station's audience—young, predominantly male—is attracted to bold, strong graphics. The odd shaped areas of black and white, the reversed type and the geometric display face in the masthead fit the bill. Instead of line breaks between paragraphs, run-ins set in Futura Extra Bold signal the beginnings of paragraphs. It's a popular device in publications that target young readers and helps keep the block of copy tightly together.

Insignia has a gritty, industrial quality that is frequently seen on promotional materials for contemporary groups and stations that lean more toward hard rock. Futura Extra Bold takes on the character of its surroundings again, looking geometric and assertive here. The Times Roman body copy ensures readability. It also gives the piece some softness and warmth to prevent it from having a heavy metal look.

Masthead: Insignia 106 pt. and Futura Extra Bold 12 pt., horizontal scaling: 150%

Heads: Futura Extra Bold 12/14, horizontal scaling: 150%

Table of Contents Numbers: Futura Extra Bold 24 pt., horizontal scaling: 150%

Table of Contents Copy: Futura 14/24

Body: Times 12/16 with Futura Extra Bold 12/16 run-ins

Pull Quote: Futura Extra Bold 16/24

Elegant Simplicity

The elegance of this furniture store ad is enhanced by the use of a script face for the headline, restraint and simplicity in the treatment of descriptive copy, and lots of white space. The formal symmetry of the ad is appropriate for fine furniture in traditional styles; it conveys not only a feeling of elegance but of order and fine craftsmanship.

Snell, unlike most scripts, is not overly ornate and is relatively legible even when reversed. It has a black tie quality that implies class and elegance. Futura's simple letterforms and light color (just dark enough to hold up over the background screen or tint) make it a good choice for the brief body copy.

Headline: Snell 126 pt.
Body: Futura 11/22

Bold, Clean

A stencil-style display face is perfect for a warehouse sale for almost any client, a stock merchandise ad for a wholesale or discount store, or a crate-themed ad for an importer or produce store/market. This slightly condensed version of Futura Black is more sophisticated than most stencil-style faces and gives the ad a bold impact. (When set with more open letterspacing and/or curved around a border, this same face can look delicate and create an entirely different mood.)

The bold type used for product names and prices defines the beginnings and the ends of each paragraph of copy. The "read-ins," generous leading for the sell copy, and the ample white space give this ad a clean, upscale look rather than the "bargain basement" look produced by packing every inch of the ad with copy. Two weights of Helvetica are used to create the "read-ins" and body copy. Sticking with one family keeps the ad cleaner than mixing a serif and a sans serif in this case.

Headline: Futura Black 106 pt., horizontal scaling: 80%
Prices on Photos: Helvetica Ultra Compressed 18 pt.
Body: Helvetica and Helvetica Black 12/18

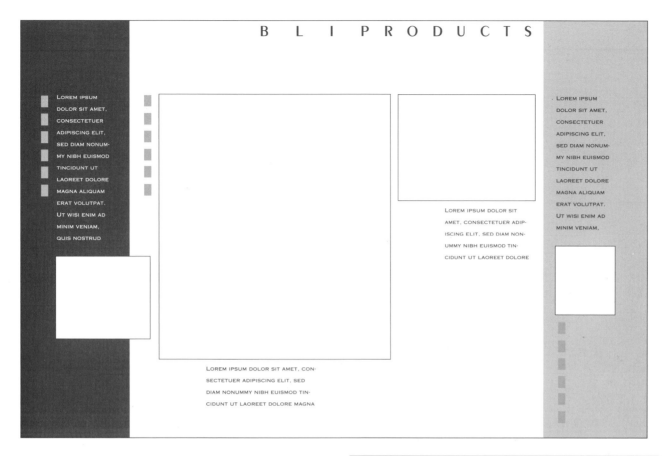

Lorem ipsum dolor sit amet, consectetuer adipiscing elit, sed diam nonummy nibh euismod tincidunt ut laoreet dolore magna aliquam erat volutpat. Ut wisi enim ad minim veniam, quis nostrud

Lorem ipsum dolor sit amet, consectetuer adipiscing elit, sed diam nonummy nibh euismod tincidunt ut laoreet dolore

Lorem ipsum dolor sit amet, consectetuer adipiscing elit, sed diam nonummy nibh euismod tincidunt ut laoreet dolore magna

Lorem ipsum dolor sit amet, consectetuer adipiscing elit, sed diam nonummy nibh euismod tincidunt ut laoreet dolore magna aliquam erat volutpat. Ut wisi enim ad minim veniam,

Digital

There are a variety of computer-generated or bitmapped fonts available for display type on a brochure for a computer-related product or service. This bitmapped type was created by printing Chicago with font substitution turned off in the page layout program. (The best known, deliberately bitmapped font is Oakland, created by Emigre.)

Generous and erratic tracking and kerning also conjure up a mental image of a computer screen as does reversed out type (despite the advent of WYSIWYG screens). Copperplate Gothic suggests the small, all caps type produced by some computers. Copperplate is available only in all caps; it is, therefore, less readable than uppercase and lowercase, so it must be used with care. Keep the word count to a minimum and the line lengths short as shown here.

Cover

Head: Chicago 36/70, tracking: +153, manual line and letterspacing
Subhead: Exotica 350 24/70, tracking: +153, manual line and letterspacing

Interior

Head: Exotica 350 30/70, tracking: +18
Body and Captions: Copperplate Gothic 10/22

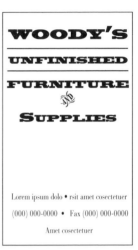

Old-Fashioned, Warm

Display type with an antique flavor can be appropriate for any client with a traditional business or service who wants to project old-fashioned charm and warmth. Woodtype faces can be especially effective for pubs, inns, shipping lines, lumber yards and thrift stores. Many type houses offer a nice variety of styles for both traditional and digital typography, and there are clip art books of alphabets that you can scan in and rework.

Blackoak has a rough-hewn quality that suggests woodworking. It's a large, dark face, so try to give it ample room to breathe. The other information shouldn't try to compete with this powerful logo, but it must stand out on the page well enough to be easily found. Bauer Bodoni has a nineteenth century look, but it is softer than the Blackoak. Although Bodoni is not a dark face, it has enough color not to get lost on the page.

Letterhead Sheet

Logotype: Blackoak 27/30, 18/30 and 19/30—sizes set to width—the ampersand is a 36 pt. woodtype ornament
Address and Phone/Fax: Bauer Bodoni 9 pt.

Business Card

Logotype: Blackoak 19/26, 13/26 and 14/26—sizes set to width—the ampersand is a 24 pt. woodtype ornament
Address, Name and Phone/Fax: Bauer Bodoni 9/18

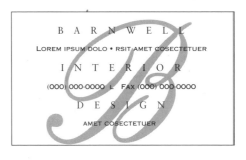

Elegant, Romantic

For a more elegant and classic or romantic look, a script face is a good choice. The single initial *B* here acts as a monogram and conveys a sense of formality. It implies that the client has good taste and high standards. To ensure even placement of the type, the three lines of the client's name were placed first and the other copy fit between them.

Embassy has ornamental but not ornate letterforms. The strokes are heavy enough that the letterform can still be distinguished when it has been screened back to run behind the type on the business card. Sabon's flared serifs, classic proportions and delicate letterforms make it appear to flow from the script *B*. Copperplate Gothic has the look of traditional engraving, which makes it a natural for this classic, formal look.

Letterhead Sheet

Logotype: Embassy 72 pt. and Sabon 14/40 caps, tracking: +50, manual letterspacing
Address and Phone/Fax: Copperplate Gothic 7 pt., tracking: +50, manual line spacing

Business Card

Monogram Letter: Embassy 180 pt.
Logotype: Sabon 14/40, tracking: +50, manual letterspacing
Address, Name and Phone/Fax: Copperplate Gothic 7 pt., tracking: +50, manual line spacing

Music in the Air Poster

Art Direction/Hand Lettering/Illustration: Eric Rickabaugh
Fonts: Linoscript, Futura, Hand Lettering
The take-off on old illustration style calls for some period typography, in this case Hand Lettering. The ornate script, colorful illustration, and the copper and gold inks give this poster a festive quality.

Remember the Alamo

Art Director: Chuck Creasy, Gregg Boling
Designer: Gregg Boling
Typography: Macography by Jeff Turner
© Chuck Creasy Creative 1990
Fonts: Heliotype, Insignia A, Madrone, Charme
This tongue-in-cheek retail announcement for Joz Cloz is a lively layout of display types, photos, and screened-back line art.

Inks on Enhance

Art Direction/Design: Eric Rickabaugh
Lettering: James Fedor
Production: Tony Meuser
© 1992 Rickabaugh Graphics
Fonts: Various and Hand Lettering
This promotion shows the results you can obtain with colored inks on colored paper from the Enhance line. Display type often serves as a graphic. Here, the letterforms of a variety of fonts create an interesting, abstract pattern. The layered letters in a variety of screens and tints, especially the swashes of a serif italic, make an attractive background.

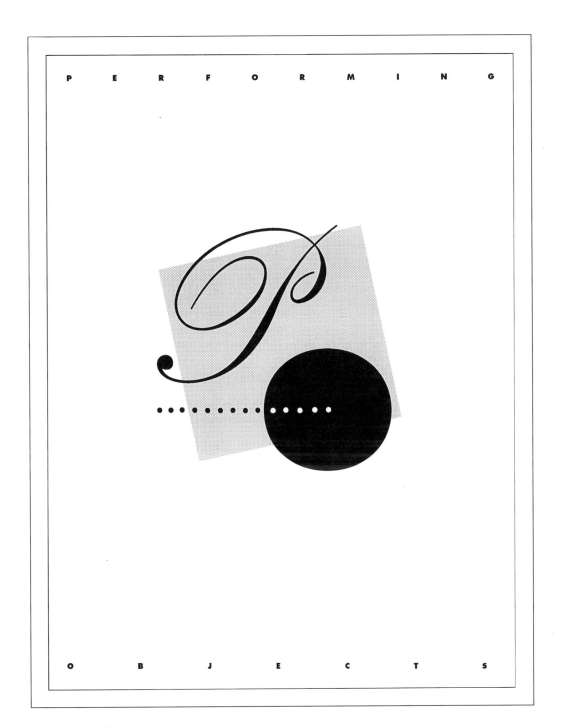

Performing Objects

Designer: David Betz

Careful placement of letters and geometric shapes are used
on this identity of a Contemporary Arts Center exhibition.

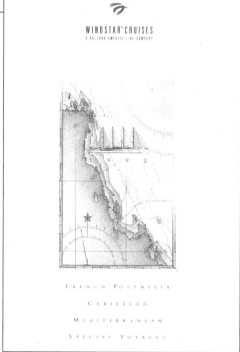

Windstar Cruises

Art Director: Jack Anderson
Designers: Denise Weir, Jack Anderson, Paula Cox
Illustrator: Bruce Morser
Fonts: Bodoni, Aurea Titling, Bank Script
The italic display face has a windswept quality. Large initial caps appear in soft pastels—aqua, sand and shell pink. Smaller initial caps are in turquoise. Instead of a delicate text, Bodoni is used. It is bold enough to be legible when set in warm gray over a cream background.

YOU KNOW HIM AS SANTA CLAUS.

Yet in France, children call him Le Père Noël. In Sweden, he appears as the tiny elf Jultomten, whose sleigh is pulled by Julbock the Christmas goat. And in Germany he is Pelze-Nicol, who wears bishop's robes and rides a white pony. Right now you can see twelve of the world's most charming Santas as the Cincinnati Zoo Festival of Lights presents "Gift Givers of the World." These life-size figures have been hand-crafted in surprising detail, and wear authentic antique costumes. These rare Santas will only be here once. So come share this unique holiday experience you won't find anywhere else. Only during the Season's Brightest Nights. Every evening, November 25 through January 1.

Cincinnati Zoo
Festival of Lights

Festival of Lights Ads
Creative Director: David Bukvic
Art Director: Teresa Newberry
Agency: Mann Bukvic
Fonts: Nicholas Cochin
The holidays provide an opportunity to use nostalgic engravings and decorative type and border treatments reminiscent of illuminated manuscripts.

DAILY DEPARTURES FOR CHRISTMAS PAST.

The steam whistle bellows its familiar song, and with a churn of the wheels, you are fast on your way to a Christmas straight from Currier and Ives. You'll wind through a park adorned in the colors of the season, as a horse-drawn carriage passes by. A collection of hand-crafted Santas will tell of rich Christmas traditions all over the world. And everywhere you look, shimmering lights brighten the night like a million fiery stars. The enchanted train awaits you. Join us soon at the Festival of Lights. The Season's Brightest Nights. Every evening, November 25 through January 1.

Cincinnati Zoo
Festival of Lights

Beyond the Rules

Some designers seek—or maybe just find—type solutions that challenge their audience. The rules will produce what the client expects: legible, clear, well-organized or logically prioritized material. It will have the mood or style that the audience has come to expect from this organization, product and format. This is a sound, sensible approach when the audience has definite expectations of how the printed piece will look and read, when it's critical that the information be read, and when you're trying to inspire confidence or trust in the audience or the client. It can be a good solution but it will, to at least some extent, be predictable.

The inspiration for new approaches comes from a variety of sources and requires that you let go of a lot of preconceived notions—and often client directives—and push the type to the limit.

Communication doesn't result only from reading copy; it occurs on many levels. Your type treatment may approach communication visually or emotionally. Slick typography can blunt the impact of your message and even evoke cynicism. Often a crude, rough approach is the best for a simple, direct statement.

Sometimes words aren't enough, no matter how well they're designed and set. If you feel that you can't coax, lead, trick or force your audience to read the client's sales copy, present a strong image instead. (It may not be what's said but how it's said that matters.) Some designers are even questioning the necessity for legibility. They feel that readers become more involved with copy they have to puzzle out and are, therefore, more likely to read all of it.

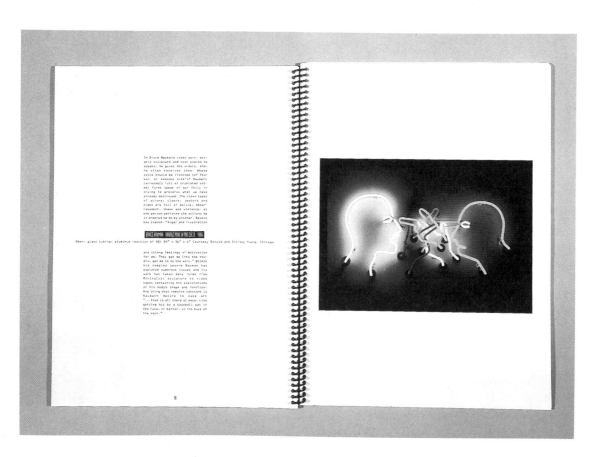

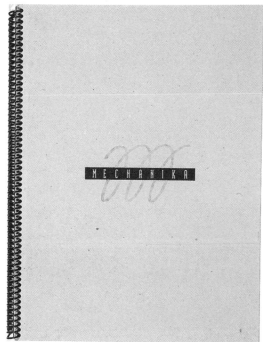

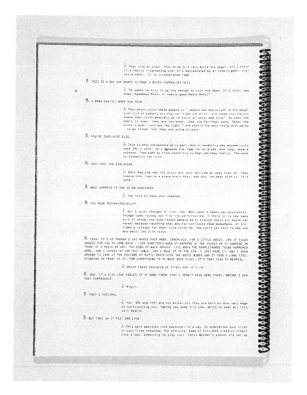

Mechanika

Designer: David Betz

Photographer: Ron Forth

This spare, graphic approach is used for a catalog for a Contemporary Arts Center exhibit of machine-based imagery. The choppy rhythm of the text doesn't enhance readability, but it reinforces the theme.

impression

Print communications work the same way. The look

of a piece creates an impression that influences

whether or not it will be read. Therefore, it's critical

that every communication conveys a *message* that

supports its content and intended response

        through appropriate design,

        well-crafted writing,

        carefully selected paper

        and quality printing

no matter how small the budget is.

    At *First Impression* we want to help you

make lasting, impactful impressions with your

communications, particularly those that don't

require four-color printing. We produce only one-, two-

and three-color printing and we do it mindful of ⑤

and ⏰ restrictions. We've created *Impression* in

the hopes of broadening your understanding of the

potential that can be achieved with quality one-, two-

and three-color communications. We hope you enjoy

this and coming issues.

    First Impression

    Printers and Lithographers, Inc.

    795 Touhy Avenue

    Elk Grove, Illinois 60007

    312.439.8600

WHAT COLOR IS A SMILE?

Think of a child's euphoric smile. Would it mean the same thing to you if it were green or blue? Are you actually seeing the same color as others do when you look at a particular smile? Can two people see and interpret the same rhapsodically red smile in the same way?

The music of color resonates in every area of our lives and plays melodies with our emotions. Color is as much a part of our responses to life as are sounds, forms, words and pictures. From the subtlety of the shimmering rush of water in a stream to the brilliance of a startling sunset, color has the power to move us.

With careful attention, communicators can control the power of color to augment messages conveyed in print. This issue of Impression *will look at the meanings and idiosyncrasies of color so that we can consciously construct color harmonies in print communications*

The Mind Leads the Blind

    Color is like flavor (*"mmm"*)

    or odor (*"ahh"*)

    it's a physical sensation (*"oooh!"*).

In its simplest terms, the sensation of color arises when

light enters the eye and stimulates retinal cells to produce

a response, which is then transmitted to the brain. Different

wavelengths of light, combined with the quality of light

seen, causes o

The spectral cu

700, with violet

reds at the high

into perception

ences and conn

Do You See

wall in a house

by bright blue?

elicit the same

able and myster

P A T T E R N

societies over g

ple, red and gre

in our culture be

holiday for year

reinforced a par

inherently "Chr

many colors and

time, too. A cla

these particular

shape virtually

sign of safety by

individual as ea

and dislikes are

first

The way we look.

    The way we act.

    The things we say. (*"yeah"*)

The fact and fiction of how others perceive us

formulates their impressions.

    And it's that first contact

    the first impression

    that often sets the tone for

everything that follows ⇾

*"It was the Rainbow gave thee birth
And left thee all her lovely hues."*
W. H. Davies, The Kingfisher

First Impression

Art Director/Designer: Mark Oldach
Fonts: Goudy, Futura, Helvetica Ultra Condensed Light
This promotional brochure for First Impression Printers and Lithographers takes an indirect approach with engaging copy rather than a more direct sales pitch. The audience of graphic arts professionals and designers will enjoy the wit and the bit of color theory presented in a clean, careful type treatment.

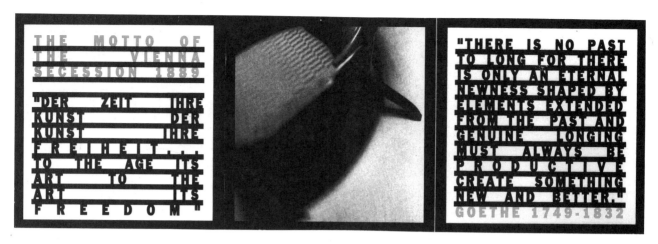

Secession

Art Director: John Pylypczak, Diti Katona
Designer: John Pylypczak
Photographer: Karen Levy
Fonts: Franklin Gothic, Bodoni

The designers drew on political billboards for this strong, graphic type solution on a folder and other collateral pieces promoting an Austrian line of modern furniture called "Secession." The piece ties the motto of the Vienna Secession in 1889 as stated by Goethe to a similar quote by the furniture designer through typographic design.

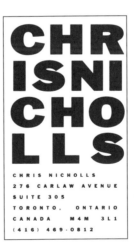

Chris Nicholls

Art Director: Diti Katona, John Pylypczak

Designer: John Pylypczak

Fonts: Franklin Gothic, Franklin Gothic Heavy

Unconventional scale and a play on black-and-white (negatives) with type creates a distinctive look on this folder, flyer and cards for a photographer.

Writing that peels

back the skin of

society to find its

politics, its heart.

words too

raw to sit

on the

page

Closer Look Passport

Art Director: Mark Oldach
Designer: Don Emery
Fonts: Letter Gothic, Snell Roundhand, Sabon
This brochure for an international U.S./French film copro-
duction mixes photography and still video images. Running
explanatory copy is reversed out of a bar across the top of
the pages; although the type is quite small, it still has
enough presence to be found and read. Provocative snippets
of copy are superimposed on the photos in different typefaces and sizes seemingly at random. But there is, in fact, a
careful, thoughtful integration of typography and visuals.

Add a Little Magic

Concept/Design: Rick Valicenti

Digital Imagery: Mark Rattin, Tony Klassen

Typography: Richard Weaver, Rick Valicenti

© 1992 Thomas Munroe, Inc.

Fonts: Meta Bold, Meta Caps, Swift Regular

This brochure uses state-of-the-art computer images to impress the sophisticated target audience. Type becomes a visual design element, too. The topics for each course, set in reversed lines of varying lengths, are grouped into intriguing shapes. Type works with color to emphasize the benefits of attending a particular course. The course description is an uppercase and lowercase setting of a serif face in a yellow box, while the copy that calls out the benefit is set in an all caps, sans serif against white.

Index